part asian · 100% hapa

Portraits by Kip Fulbeck

Foreword by Sean Lennon

Afterword by Paul Spickard

CHRONICLE BOOKS

SAN FRANCISCO

Library of Congress Cataloging-in-Publication Data available.

ISBN 0-8118-4959-7

Manufactured in China.

Design by Jonathan Cecil and Kip Fulbeck
Digital Compositing by Derrick Velasquez and Michael Velasquez

Distributed in Canada by Raincoast Books
9050 Shaughnessy Street
Vancouver, British Columbia V6P 6E5

10 9 8 7 6 5 4 3 2 1

Chronicle Books LLC
85 Second Street
San Francisco, California 94105

www.chroniclebooks.com

ha•pa (hä'pä) *adj.* **1.** *Slang.* of mixed racial heritage with partial roots in Asian and/or Pacific Islander ancestry. **n. 2.** *Slang.* a person of such ancestry. [*der.*/Hawaiian: *Hapa Haole* (half white)]

acknowledgments

This project involved several thousand people over three years, via organization, communication, participation, and production. I wish to thank everyone involved, and to mention several in particular.

Thanks to my family for their continued love and support, to Hapa Issues Forum for their steadfast devotion to promoting Hapa awareness, and to Mikyla Bruder, Brett MacFadden, Alan Rapp, Bridget Watson Payne, and the amazing staff at Chronicle Books for their commitment to producing innovative work.

Thanks to my friends Keith Alexander, Lindsay Castro, Jonathan Cecil, Willy Chui, Mary Clark, Casey Copeland, Jenn Crawford, Wei-Ming Dariotis, Jen Diskin, Rebecca Drexler, Kristina Fredriksson, Tejvir Grewall, Amy Hill, Robert Horsting, Stewart David Ikeda, Matt Kelley, Ming-yan Lai, Jaker Lemberger, Sean Lennon, Ronnie Lin, Heather Milne, Cindie Nakashima, Vicki Nam, Victoria Namkung, Dan Nazaretta, Jocelyn Nguyen, Ben Northover, "Marky" Mark Pasadilla, Joe Perez, Harry Reese, Joel Sherman, Paul Spickard, Phel Steinmetz, Kellie Stoelting, Kevin Tam,

Andres Torres, LeeAnn Trusela, Derrick Velasquez, Michael Velasquez, and Teresa Williams-Léon.

I also wish to express my gratitude to the Department of Art, the Interdisciplinary Humanities Center, and Academic Senate at the University of California, Santa Barbara; to my agent, Faye Bender; to my research assistants, Krista Bergenstal, Lizvet Corral, Jean Lee, Tracey On, and Jaclyn Tamizato; and to Lynda Barry and Jim Goldberg for inspiration.

Finally, thanks to all the generous people who opened their homes, schools, and workplaces for us to photograph in, and to all the Hapa participants and supporters throughout the country. Your belief in the project made this book possible.

Kip Fulbeck
Santa Barbara, CA

introduction | kip fulbeck

"You don't look Chinese."

A random time, a random place, and I'm still here. I know this routine inside out. I've got it memorized, can do it blindfolded. If I answer "English" or "Irish," I'll get the "No, what *else* are you?" response. If I answer "Part Chinese," it's more along the lines of "Yeah, I can see it in your . . . (insert physical feature)." And if I answer "American," I'm in for a longer conversation than I'm usually in the mood for.

What are you?

I answer the question every day of my life—depending on the day itself, the location, my hair, or what I'm eating or doing. I get mistaken for Native American, Filipino, Hawaiian, African American (especially when my head is shaved), Mexican, Cuban, Middle Eastern, Indian . . . I've listened to a black woman chastise me for denying my African heritage and a First Nations member push me to register my status. I'm greeted in Spanish, Farsi, and pidgin, all the while being escorted to the various back tables in various Chinese restaurants and handed forks (the long hair, non-Gucci, tattoo tables—the *brown* tables). On the street, interracial couples approach and scrutinize my face, wondering out loud what their future child may look like, and I learned to smile back when they do it. They're just curious, right?

Our country is lazy. And I'm not talking about obesity levels. I'm talking "whatever." We're uncomfortable with people who don't fit neatly into boxes because when they don't do so, it requires effort on our part. It's easier to keep things uncomplicated, trouble free. We ask people how they're doing when most of the time we don't really want to know. We follow meeting someone with questions like "So, what do you do?" and expect simple and easy answers. More than that, we usually give simple and easy answers when defining our own lives, generally doing so in terms of vocation. How bizarre is that? We can't give a straight answer to the what-kind-of-music-do-you-like question (note: answering "everything" here is a cop-out), but we'll happily label ourselves with "real estate," "pharmacist," "construction," "IT," or "television." I'm no different here. I work as an artist, a writer, a performer, a teacher, a lifeguard—but I know it's easier to just say "professor." People treat me better, and it makes my mother happy. I might even get a better table in the Chinese restaurant. Might.

Compartmentalization is easy, even inviting. At the individual level, we create distinct and telling titles of association—delineating our personal relationships into "business," "family," or "social" when the categories and personal relationships themselves continually blur and redefine. (How many of us raise our eyebrows when our partner mentions a new "friend"?) It's the same at the global level, when we cheer our own country's Olympic athletes rather than the pushing of human accomplishment, when we reduce the complexities of foreign policy into "good" and "evil." Our country and its individuals continually seek out absolutes and simplicity, when absolutes don't exist. Besides, absolutes, to be honest, aren't all that interesting.

What's interesting is ambiguity. What's interesting is the haziness, the blurrings, the undefinables, the space and tension between people, the area between the margins that pushes us to stop, to question. Hapas know the question inside out. *What are you?* And we know we can't answer it any more than we can choose one body part over another. We love the question. We hate the question. And we know many times people aren't satisfied with our answers. (In my case, the only people who tell me I'm *not* Chinese are Chinese people—including most of my relatives.) For what it's worth, I stopped checking "Chinese" on the ethnicity question somewhere in my teens, on the same day I decided I wanted to be both accurate and honest. It just made sense. I figured if I didn't fit in a box—whether on a job application, school form, health questionnaire, or arrest record (another story), then I wasn't going to lie to make myself fit it anymore. I figured it's the box idea that needed to change.

Twenty years later and not much is different. A few small steps here and there: at thirty-five, I was allowed to answer the U.S. Census accurately for the first time; scores of Hapa celebrities now permeate popular film, television, print, music, and sports; millions of us out there and growing . . . I look at these facts and I can't figure it out. How can mainstream Hapa awareness still be almost nonexistent? Why is "multiracial" still limited to a black/white paradigm in the national mind-set? Is it simply because until now Hapas had no title, no name, no way to even identify as a group? Is it because so many of us never thought about or cared about it ourselves, never considering ourselves part of something larger? Were some of us reluctant to even acknowledge our ever-expanding group of similarly mixed individuals, pleased in our role as the special one, the exotic one—or conversely, content to blend in and *pass*? As many answers exist as individuals. I knew starting this project that I would uncover more questions than I could ever answer. I also knew that's why I wanted to do it.

Like many Hapa children, I thought I was the only one. Certainly, interracial marriages were uncommon for my parents' generation, even frowned upon in many communities and outlawed in many states until 1967. Yet more than simply being uncommon, the idea of multiraciality was fundamentally ignored in popular culture. Growing up in the late seventies, my only vague media reference to multiraciality was Mr. Spock from *Star Trek* (and that was a bit of a stretch). And while my parents fostered me in a loving and supportive home, they chose not to discuss my multiraciality with me. Perhaps they didn't recognize the issue, or did so and chose to reduce it. Or perhaps they simply had no example, no resources or tools with which to start. I can give a lot of reasons why I started this project, but when it comes down to it, I'm really making the book I wish I had access to growing up.

In second grade, we do a class exercise. Each of us has to put his or her initials on a series of small paper flags attached to pushpins. One by one, we get called to approach a wallpaper map of the world spanning the entire length of the classroom and are told to pin our initialed flags to the countries of our origins. Small Western European countries like England and Ireland quickly fill up with brightly colored flags, while the Americas, Africa, and Asia remain untouched. When my turn comes, I walk up to the same countries and squeeze my pins into the common England and Ireland piles, then walk what seems like a mile across the class and place my last flag in China. Mine is the only flag outside Western Europe. A couple of classmates snicker and I sit down. It's thirty years later and I still remember the feeling. I see it in slow motion. If there's a better way to visually isolate a kid in class, let me know. But would it be that way now? It's a different time now, a different place. Would there be laughter? What would be our exercise?

My idea for this book started simply—to photograph a couple hundred Hapas and have them write about themselves. Give them the opportunity to show their image and respond in their own words to the question that accompanies the lives of us in-betweens like a second skin.

What are you?

I photographed every participant similarly—unclothed from the collarbone up, and without glasses, jewelry, excess makeup, or purposeful expression. Basically, I wanted us to look like *us*, as close to our natural selves as possible. More than eight hundred participants volunteered over several dozen shoots across the United States, many traveling several hours to be part of the project. I had individuals self-designate their ethnic backgrounds to be printed and paired with their images, a strategy I chose to demystify the entire phenotype question by eliminating the mystery itself—how can you keep guessing if the answer is right there? At the same time, it was also a strategy I chose to purposely celebrate the fact that we *do* love finding out what each other's heritage is. In many ways, we're the most interested of all. The photo shoots themselves were electric (which is what happens when you throw a bunch of Hapas in a room together). People arrive excited. Surrounded by others of a common thread, the what-are-you question loses its baggage, its suspicion, its various political ramifications. In this scenario, it gets used with assertion, with claim. "Name That Asian" becomes *our* game.

What I've loved about doing this project is the surprises. I love a black/white woman in New York telling me, "Hey, I'm Hapa, too. We all came from one giant continent originally, right?" I love a San Francisco shoot where I show up and fifty people are at the door before we open. I love celebrities being excited about participating. I love repeatedly hearing the phrase "It's about time." And I love the fact that kids don't seem to care as much about the issue as adults. Maybe it's just overly excited parents combined with kids who would rather be outside playing or inside playing. Or maybe it's a different time, a different place. So what's our next exercise? I want to play too.

One exercise begins with realization. We recognize a phenomenon around us, but until now it has been nameless. The new face of the millennium is part Asian/Pacific Islander. Modeling agencies clamor to sign the next Devon Aoki or Tyson Beckford. We watch Keanu Reeves, listen to Norah Jones, cheer Tiger Woods, read Aimee Liu, and get our news from Ann Curry. *Time Magazine Asia* goes so far as to call Hapas "the poster children for 21st-century globalization." That's a lot of expectation placed upon a group that's been ignored for centuries. And now it's our time because we're in vogue? The way I look at it, it's always been our time.

foreword | sean lennon

When we are born we have no concept of what we are. It isn't until we begin biting things that we start to discern between what is and isn't us. This table? Not me. This blanket? Not me. This foot? Ouch! I guess that's me. So our sense of self develops. I am this foot. I am this hand. I am this mouth. I am not this carpet. I am not this table. I am . . . well, hungry.

As we grow up our sense of self becomes more complex. I am seven. I am a boy. I am in school and I am bored. Despite being boring, however, school can be an excellent place to refine one's sense of self. I am good at math. I am bad at sports. I am disliked by girls. I am loved by my mother. I am not exactly what my friends refer to as "white" or "yellow," but I am certainly not "black." Well then, what are you?

It is only human to want to belong to a group. For when humans first descended from the trees, we were, unlike today, prey for hungry saber-toothed tigers. Running from tigers gave us a sense of community and purpose. As civilization evolved we stopped running away from tigers and started running away from each other. This gave us a sense of national pride. I am English, what are you? I am a Viking, bang! You're dead!

In this melting pot we call the Technological Age, it is easier and easier to find the group to which we belong. If you are a bisexual hermaphrodite Trekkie, all you have to do is go to bisexualhermaphroditetrekkies.com to find others just like you. And so it is for that most obscure breed of non-Asian Asians known as Hapas. What does it mean to be a Hapa? All I can tell you is being a Hapa means you're not completely Asian, you're not completely Caucasian, you could be Eurasian, you could get beaten up by the Ku Klux Klan, and you will not be invited to any skinhead national pride parades anytime soon. In fact, only recently have you been recognized as anything at all. If, like me, you are half-Japanese and half-English, you will in Japan be considered white, and in America be considered Asian. This can be lonely at times, but it mostly makes for good conversation.

There are some who say that any separation between the inner and outer world is an illusion. Forces like gravity, electromagnetism, and reality television intertwine the atoms of our known universe like the invisible threads of some great cosmic tapestry. So if we are all one, why does it matter if you're white or yellow or both? Well, it matters when you're being degraded or insulted or ignored simply because of your ethnic identity, or lack thereof. But in the end it would serve humanity best to try to understand the ways in which we are the same, not the ways in which we are different. Let us remember, as we raise our proverbial freak flag high, that the reasons we fight racism and bigotry are to erase the stereotypes by which we have been falsely defined and to usher in a new era of peace, love, and ethnically diverse television programming.

There are about a million Hapas living in the United States. Doesn't that make us eligible for our own radio station? I'm not asking for Hapa history month, but how about a weekend? How about Keanu Reeves Appreciation Day? At the very least I propose someone writes a how-many-Hapas-does-it-take-to-screw-in-a-lightbulb joke. Think about it.

21

100% hapa

japanese, french, chinese, irish, swedish, sioux

What am I?

I am exactly the same
as every other person in 2500.

portuguese, filipino, spanish, chinese, hawaiian

I AM A PERSON who is BLESSED,
WITH VARIOUS ETHNIC ORIGINS.
I IDENTIFY Closely WITH THE
PACIFIC ISLANDER CULTURE, BECAUSE
OF THE ALOHA Spirit THAT EMBRACESS
ALL MAN KIND.

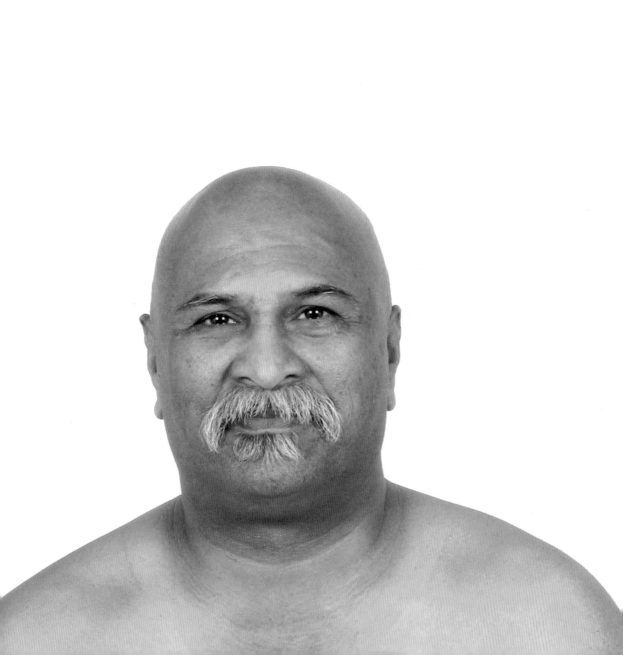

filipina, yugoslavian, norwegian, irish

I'm a girl.
I'm American.
I'm seven
I'm Hanna

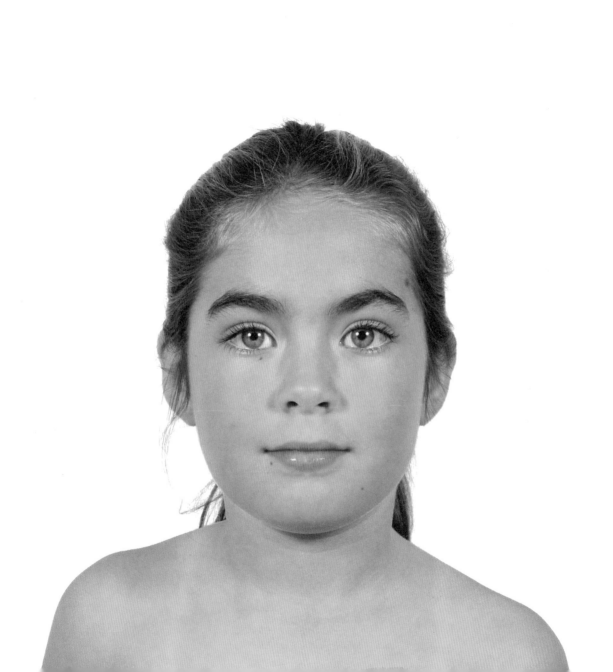

30

I am part Chinese and part Danish. I don't usually tell people I am Danish though, because they think I'm a pastry.

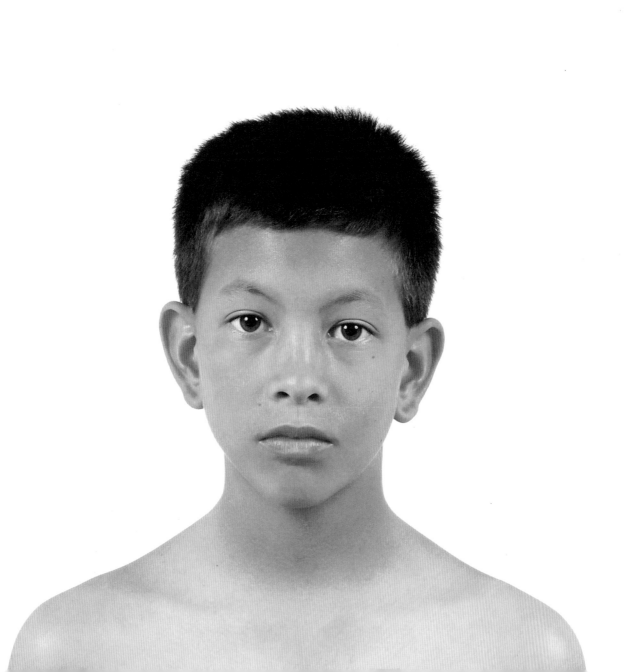

In high school I was the surly girl all in black with Nine Inch Nails lyrics scrawled across my binder...

In college I was the super-smart stoner who tried to hide from myself and anyone who loved me...

Now I'm 24, in love with life, happy to be wherever I am (unless I'm at the DMV) trying to make sense of the wonderland that is the world, maintaining a sunny disposition and a great natural tan.

32

filipino (ilocano), norwegian

34

Growing up "Hapa" in Hawaii is the essence of who I am. I was surrounded by a rainbow of nationalities. I know no other. I am culturally Hawaiian. I am the best of both worlds!

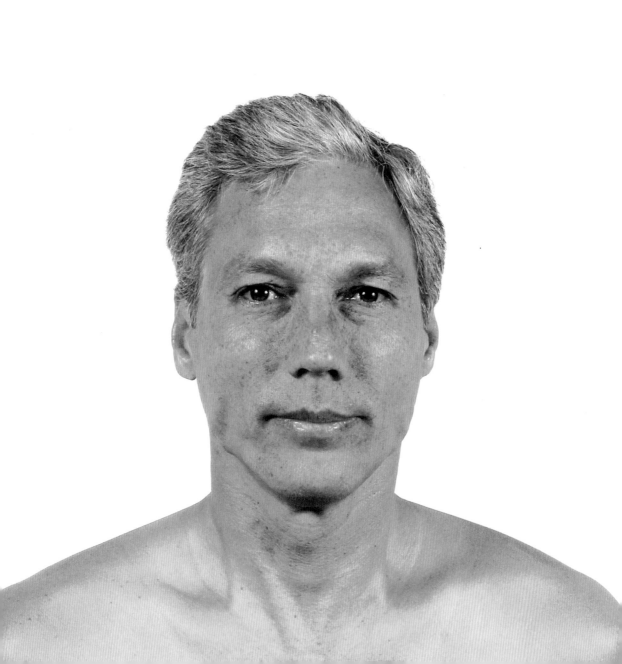

36

I am not only Indonesian
I am not exactly Dutch
I am not simply French
I am not merely German
But I am all of these combined
a representation of my ancestry
unique and proud

filipino, scottish, german

38

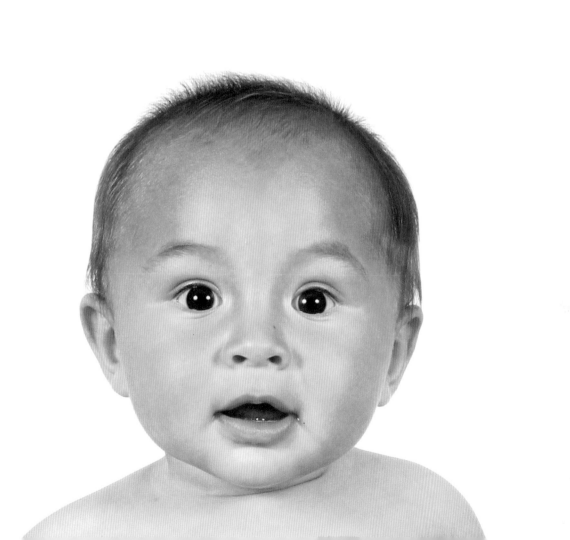

cuban, japanese, jewish

I am in 5th grade and I really like to read and write stories.
I also love to write poems, here's one of them:

40

Is it Autumn,
the brown leaves go tap top.
as they fall to the ground
Does it hurt the earth?

I wonder,

Is it Autumn?

dutch, indonesian, african american

42

I am the glowing around the moon. I am the
endless summers that you don't forget. I am the
permanent that leaves a mark.....

I am ME!!

44

I'm Karen David: a tossed salad, an insistent dreamer...
and yes, that's my real name. My middle name is Shenaz.
It means "light of the world." I always check the Other ☒ box.
I was born in a matriarchal society, among the foothills of the
Himalayas, Shillong. Meghalaya. Kids can be so mean. They'd
call me names like "Dark Ghost of China" or "Brownie",
whilst growing up in Toronto. For a long time, you couldn't
mention the "e" word (ethnic) to me, but now - all the
things I chose to hate are now the things I wanna celebrate.

46

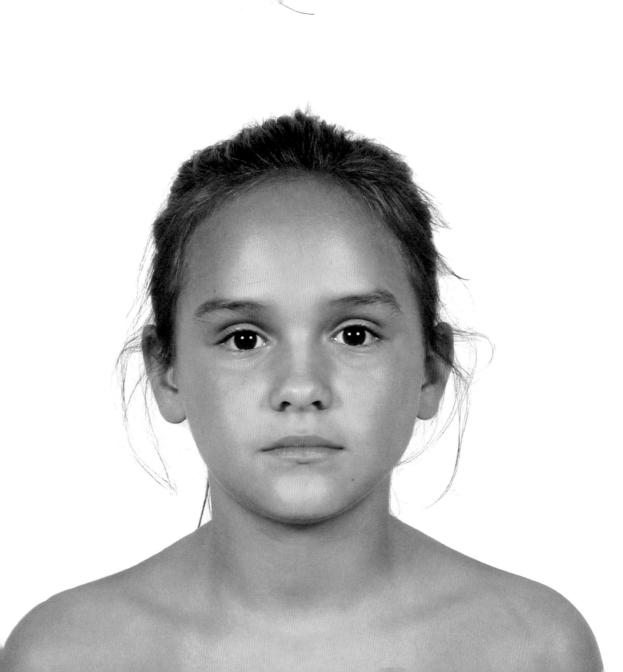

48

Washington D.C. born and raised.
I really, really like computers
and all the dorky things that
go along with it. When the
hot jams are pumping I'm
dancing. The Immaculate Collection
by Madonna is a favorite. Get
"Into The Groove" baby!

okinawan, basque, french, english, irish, dutch

50

I am a Hapa Artist.
I am a Jew who lives on Devon Avenue
in Chicago.
My Mexican Step-daughter tells me I
jump rope like a "Japanese" person
I can not say "hella" or "dope"
without sounding like a white person, ...
I have to use air-quotes.

52

I am one of three known Icelando-Thai's in existence. This has helped me blend into any group or clique and in general, has reaped me with more positives than negatives. My middle name is THOR.

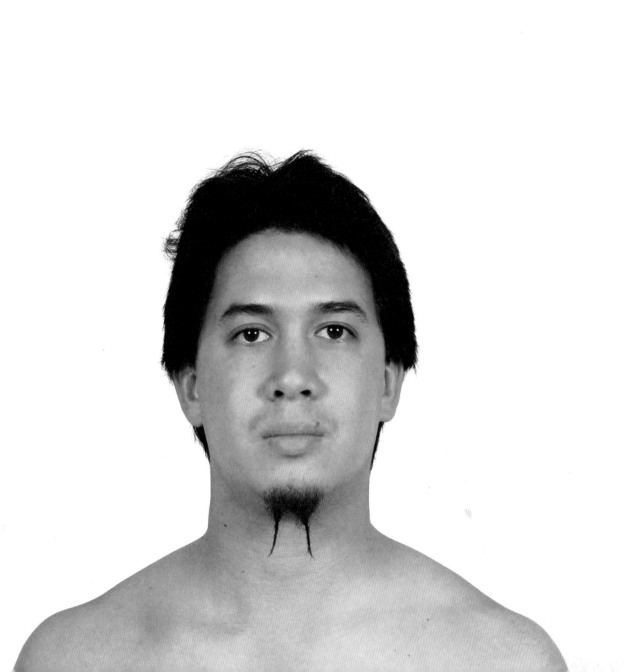

54

People can't believe I'm filipina but then I tell them I'm also norwegian, and norwegian blood can suck the color out of anything. I'm also half Irish - from both sides - my mom and dad are both half Irish. I seriously think that's all they really had in common. I grew up in a very filipino household. In family portraits with all my cousins and uncles and aunts my two brothers and I look like we're some neighbors who just dropped by for some really good food and San Miguel beer.

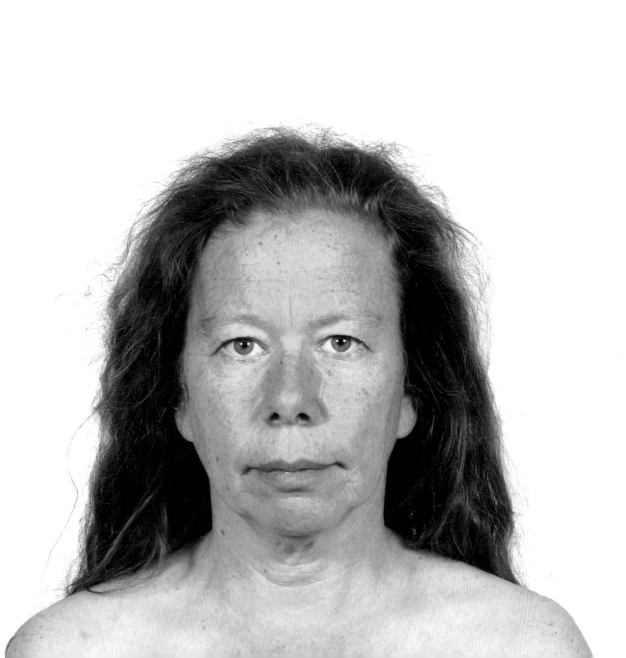

I still can't wear my hair down and feel completely comfortable. I mean, I love how it is loud and in your face but some people just can't handle it. Just like how some people can't stand that I'm Black and Pilipina American, that I'm not enough, that I don't know what it means to be Black and Pilipina American. I guess until I'm really comfortable with wearing my hair down I'm not fully expressing what it means for me to be Black and Pilipina American. So until then, I'll just keep telling people one of the few phrases that I know in Tagalog that embodies my mixed identity: Maganda ang buhok ko. I have beautiful hair.

58

chinese, vietnamese

60 I AM CONSTANTLY DEBATING WHETHER THE CHINESE HALF IS BETTER THAN THE VIETNAMESE HALF.

dutch, indonesian, french, german

62

I am Dutch Indonesian with
some German and French.
I like the fact that I keep
people guessing as to what my
ethic background is.
Growing up and as an adult
I feel like a chameleon
socially.

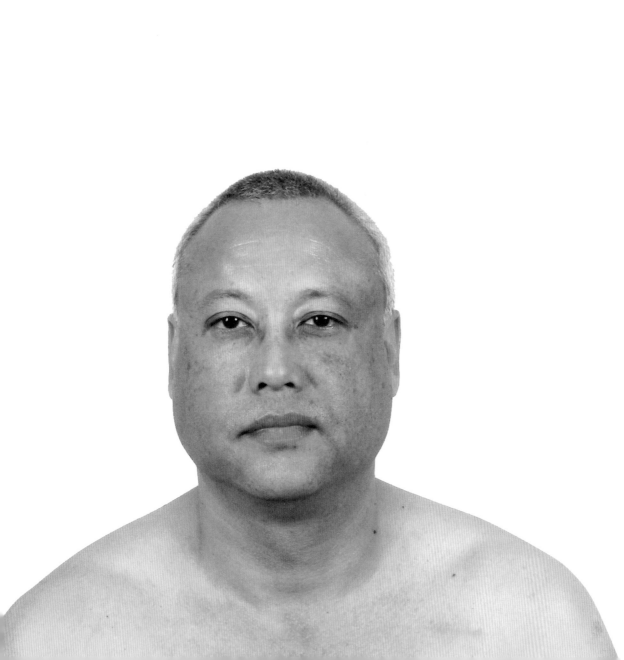

thai, mexican, irish, native american (yaqui), chinese

64

That's an interesting question for lack of a better ~~question~~ adjective — I've been asked that question many times during the course of my life. However I still have not arrived to a solid response. Based on 24 years of research I can conclude the following (in no specific order of course)

I AM	I'M NOT
Student	tall
teacher	vegetarian
daughter sister	single
funny girlfriend	left-brained
brown	lazy (most times)
moody	fitness freak
sensitive	
doodler	

DAD   MOM

I AM VERY much like both my parents

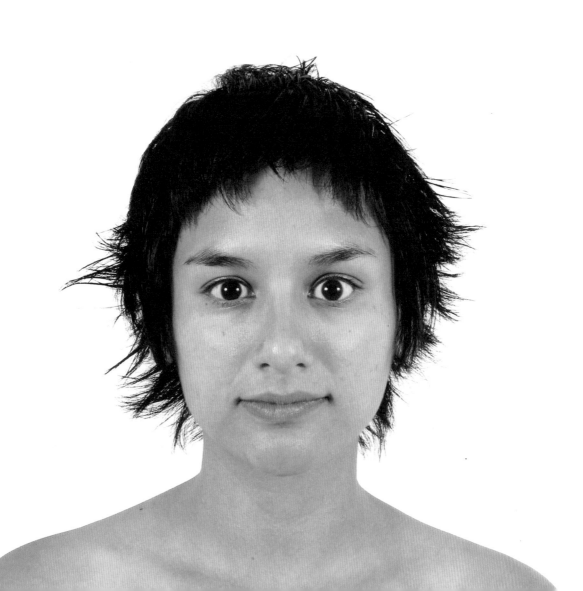

San Diego Born & Dead / JAH Worshipping /
Family Serving / Humbled Son / ONE LOVE —
Positivity Driven / Melody Moving / DIE
For the Cause / Whoever You Say I Am
or Whoever You Say I Am NoT TYPE
of Guy

filipina, hawaiian, german, polish, jewish

I couldn't answer this in a 1/2 pg!! Are you kidding?? At first it was 2 pgs, then I was told to shorten it, so then it was 1 pg... but 1/2 pg... I don't think so!! I'm Out of Control!!

what am I? I'm what's on your spoon when you pull it out of the melting Pot!!

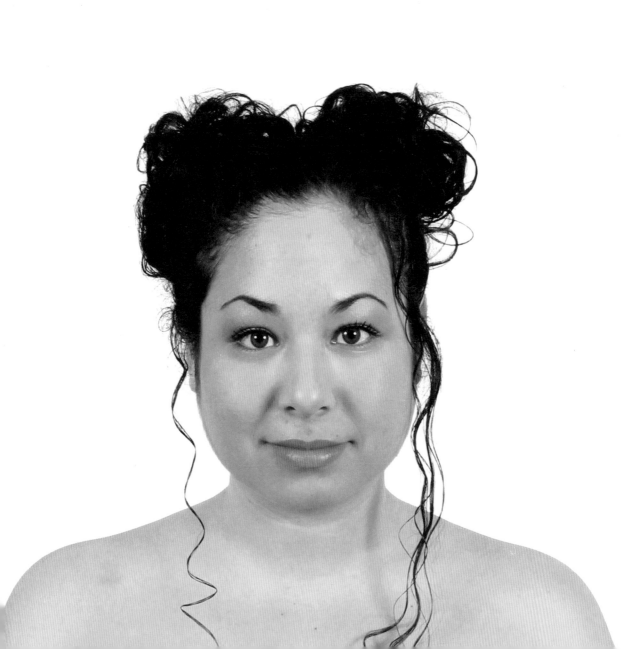

japanese, mexican, spanish, english

70

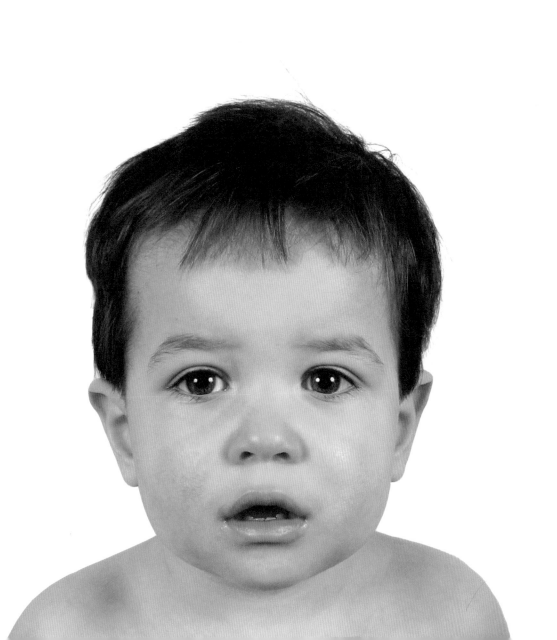

english, scottish, irish, japanese, russian, italian

72

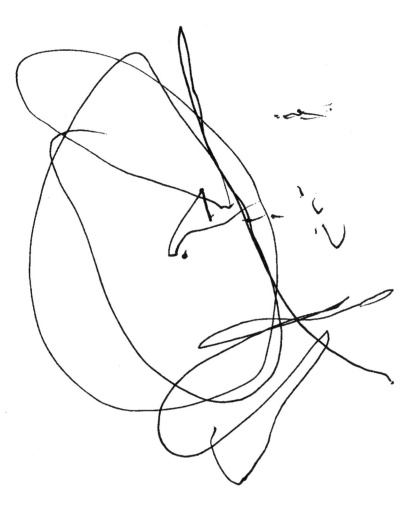

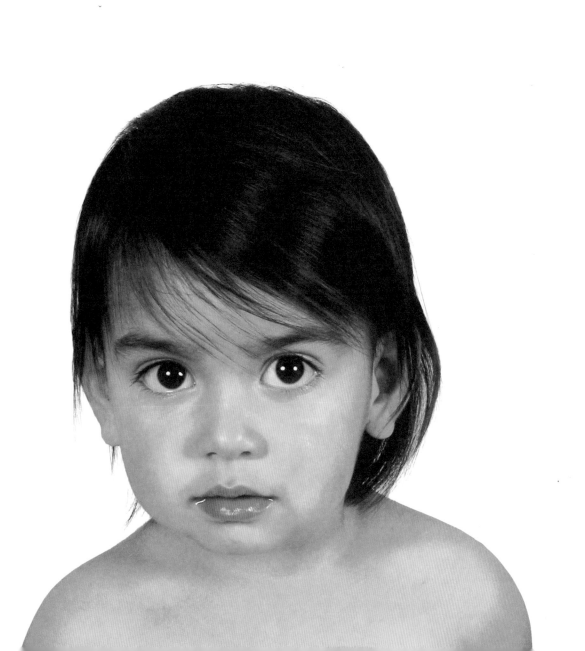

portuguese, filipina

I'm an Athletic girl And I'm very flexible.

My favorite Sport is Track. I run the 800 meter yard dash and 100 meter, 200 meter, long Jump and high Jump. During the Summer we went to maui to challenge against other Schools, and I won 7 secound and first medals. I'm very fast. Thats only when I want to run fast.

74

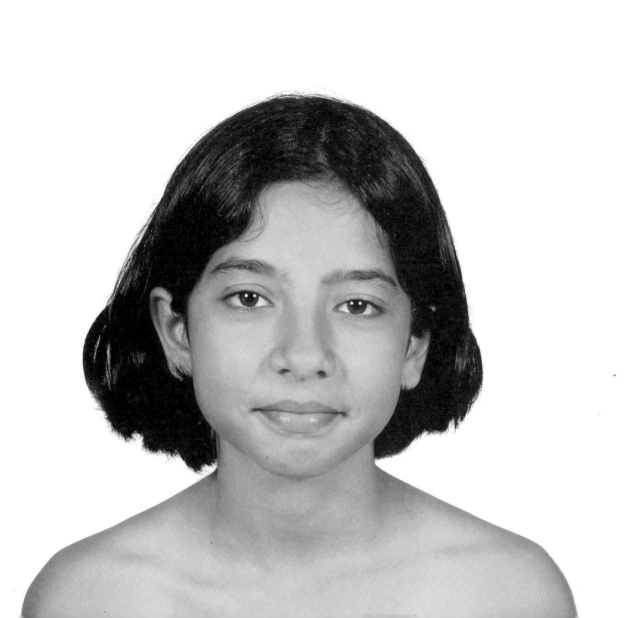

76

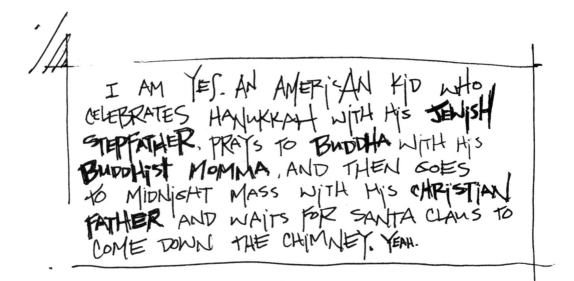

I AM YES. AN AMERICAN KID WHO CELEBRATES HANUKKAH WITH HIS **JEWISH STEPFATHER**, PRAYS TO **BUDDHA** WITH HIS **BUDDHIST MOMMA**, AND THEN GOES TO MIDNIGHT MASS WITH HIS **CHRISTIAN FATHER** AND WAITS FOR SANTA CLAUS TO COME DOWN THE CHIMNEY. YEAH.

I am circumpolar. I am many little bridges joined. My parents + grandparents have many stories of making paths, and following paths, + crossing paths. I come from whalers, trappers, adventurers, nomads — all trails led to a point: me.

80

My mother was Javanese. My Father was Dutch
My grandparents family did not want to
accept her because she was not Dutch
but later when they saw how sweet &
caring she was. everything was OK.

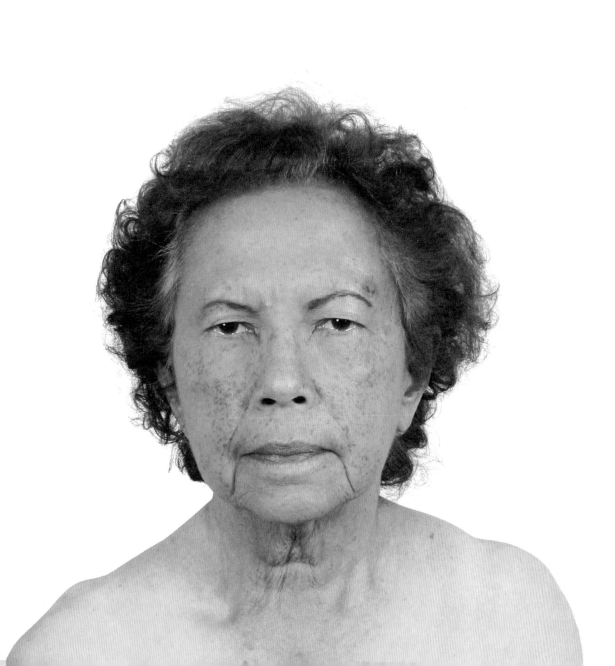

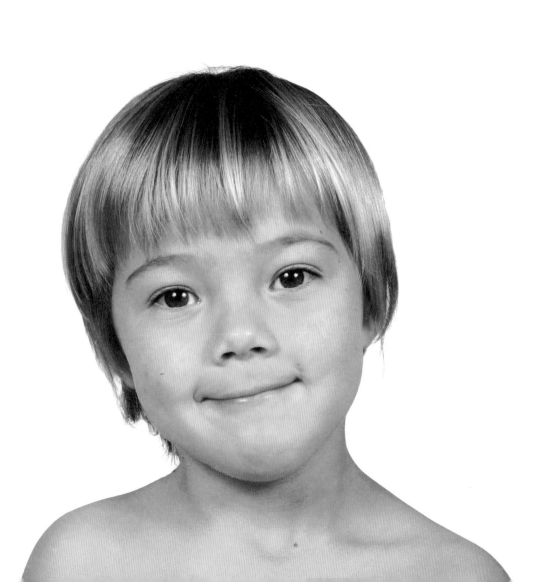

japanese, chinese, italian, german, irish, scottish, dutch

84

I am an Artist. I am an uprooted tree in full bloom of spring's wishful flowering. I'm also melodramatic.

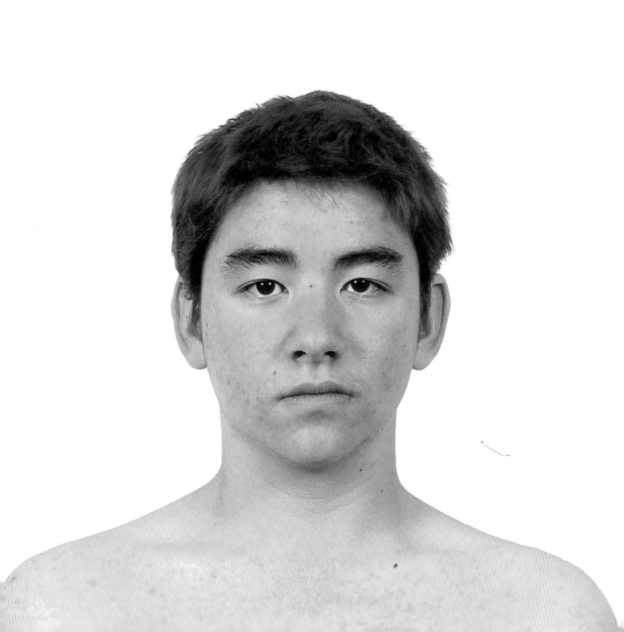

86

I'm a grown man who just exposed my breasts to a complete stranger :)

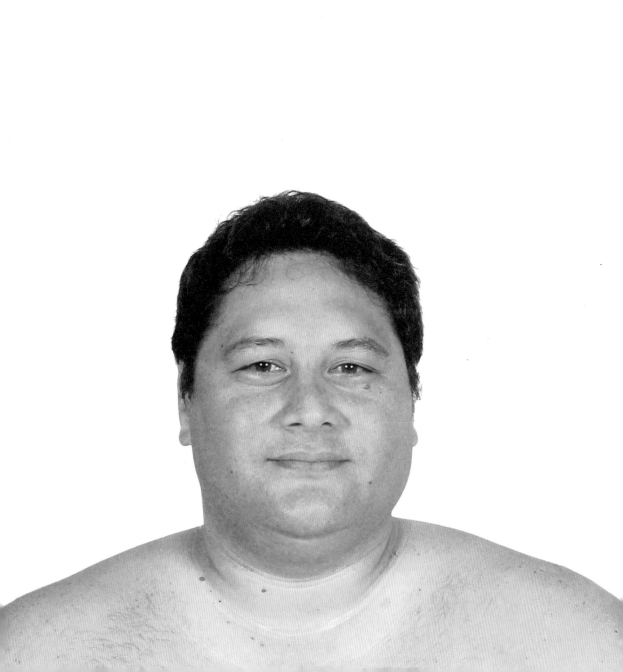

88

IF I HAD A FEW BEERS BEFORE I CAME
HERE, I WOULD KNOW WHAT TO WRITE.
I THOUGHT THIS WAS A NUDE SHOOTING SESSION.
I ACTUALLY CAME HERE TO SEE MY FRIEND KEITH
EXPOSE HIS BREAST TO A COMPLETE STRANGER.
THEY'RE BIGGER THAN MY WIFE'S!

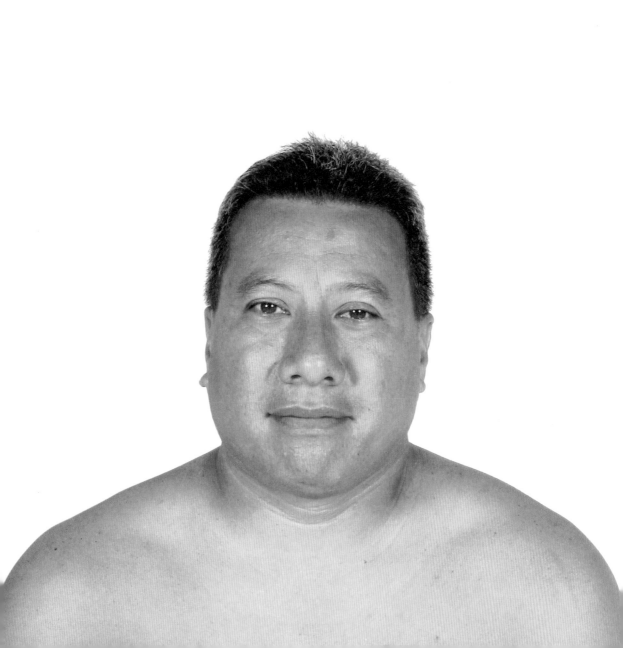

90

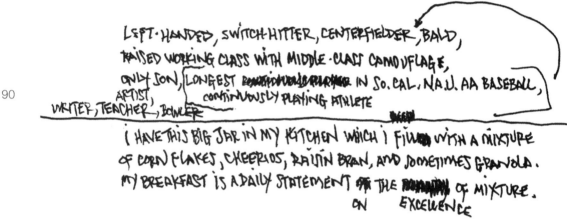

LEFT-HANDED, SWITCH-HITTER, CENTERFIELDER, BALD,
RAISED WORKING CLASS WITH MIDDLE-CLASS CAMOUFLAGE,
ONLY SON, LONGEST ~~BASEBALL PLAYER~~ IN SO. CAL. N.A.U. AA BASEBALL,
ARTIST,
WRITER, TEACHER, BOWLER
CONTINUOUSLY PLAYING ATHLETE

I HAVE THIS BIG JAR IN MY KITCHEN WHICH I FILLED WITH A MIXTURE
OF CORN FLAKES, CHEERIOS, RAISIN BRAN, AND SOMETIMES GRANOLA.
MY BREAKFAST IS A DAILY STATEMENT OF THE ~~PROBLEM~~ OF MIXTURE.
ON   EXCELLENCE

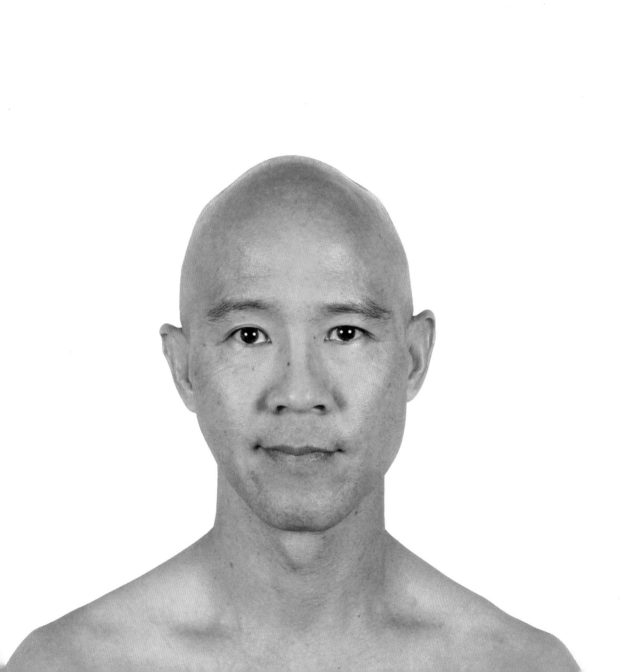

filipina, japanese, sicilian, british, polish

i am my mother's driving passion
and my father's steady reason...
...in a BATTLE TO THE DEATH.

94

I'm a strange bird,
and multi-racial although no
believes me.
I'm a ballerina, a UCSB graduate,
unemployed, and applying to grad
school.
I'm vietnamese and if you hear my
mom speak you would believe me too.
I'm scared of the real world...

thai, indian, scottish, lithuanian

Really? You don't look Thai. Well let me look again. Yeah now I can see it around your eyes. You know Thai food is my favorite. Were you born in Thailand? Do you speak, what is it, Thai-wanese? Do you dream in English or Thai-wanese? You really don't have an accent at all.

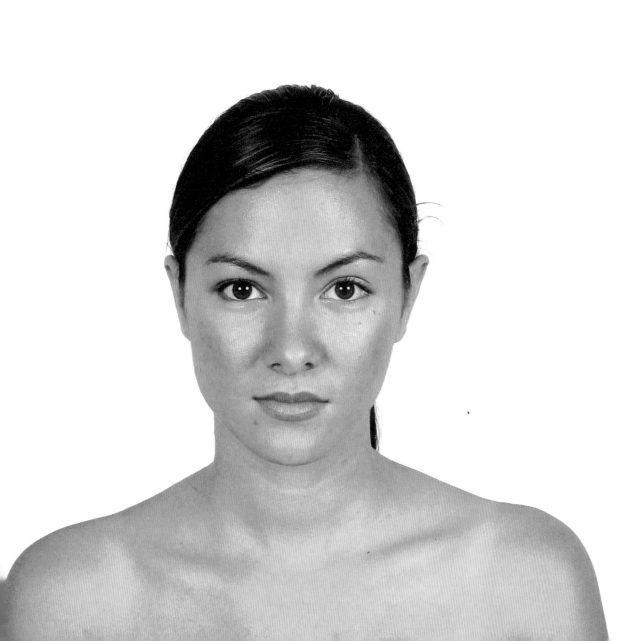

I am the dialectic of the melting pot.

I am Samurai - annoyingly arrogant, intellectually fearless, eyes trained to observe, mind to reflect. I seek communion but do not dwell on sentiment.

I am my Nisei mom's obsession to prove democracy's eventual triumph.

I am the privilege of freedom - a white man walking away from whiteness.

I am World War II. After Internment, my mom moved to Chicago where she met my WWII veteran dad. I am the world opening up. I am my parents defying war's prejudice & confusion by making babies to love.

But mostly I am "mixed". That's what we called it back in '69 when I was in sixth grade. Now I teach sixth graders, & many of them still use the term "mixed". I like being mixed. It is a good tribe to be in, & it has many brothers & sisters.

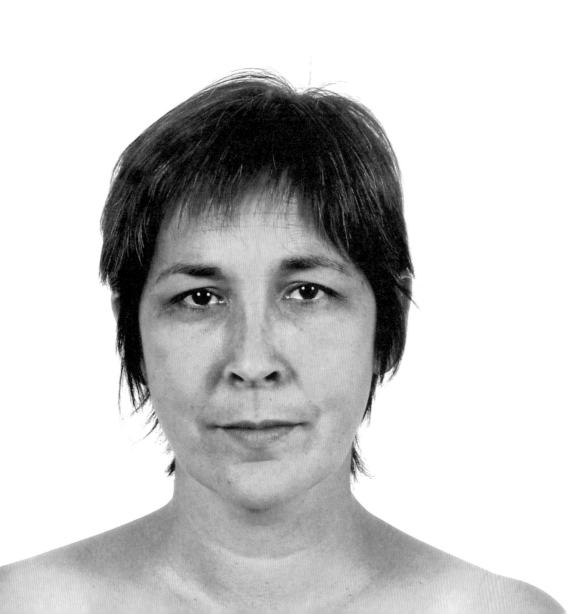

100

I make trash cans for a living, when you think trash, think of Mike! :)

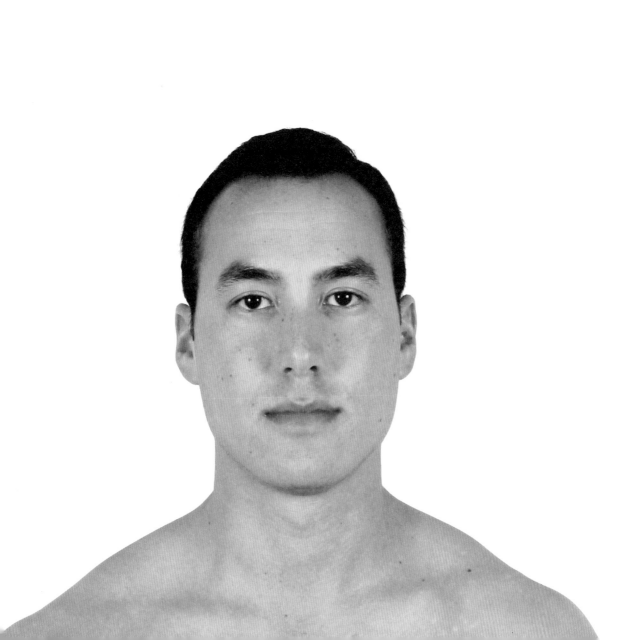

guamanian, filipino, italian, german, native american, norwegian, english

104

I'm a mixed breed multiculti cross referenced
bilingual bicoastal polymorphous smart
talkin' brainiac maniac hapa culture
vulture. I'm a New Yorker. I am
the Phoenix with no name no home flying
the compass points. I am Kate.

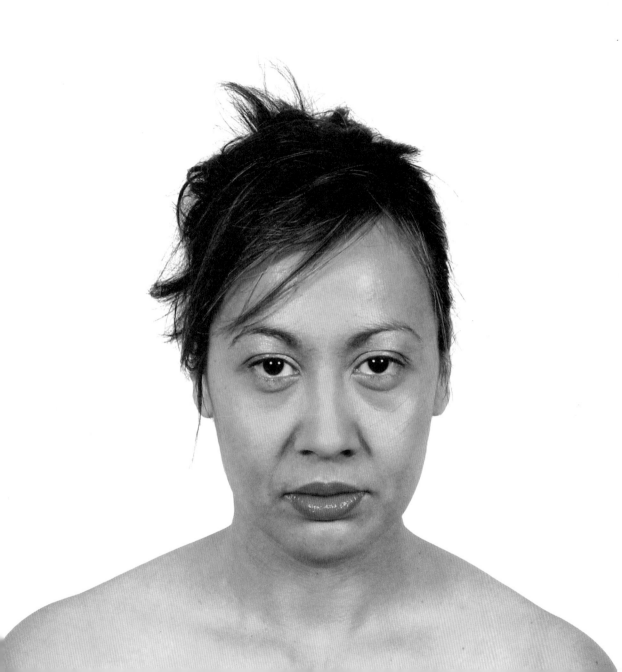

106

What am I? How should I know I'm only 17
I am not just one thing I am many all
rolled into one.
I am a girl that loves to shop.
I am a senior eagar for the future.
most people think I am just a blonde, but
I am really a brunette at heart.
I defy the rules of being a blonde.

japanese, german

108

I AM A DAILY CONTEST TO GUESS WHAT I AM.

korean, caucasian

1. Mixed race, hapa, hapa haole, Korean, Korean American, Asian, Asian American, Eurasian, half Asian, half white.

2. Vaguely flattered and vaguely threatened by your scrutiny. Okay...more flattered...Unless you get weird on me

3. Apparently more racially ambiguous than ever since growing a beard... and having ambiguous feelings about that.

4. Sleepy.

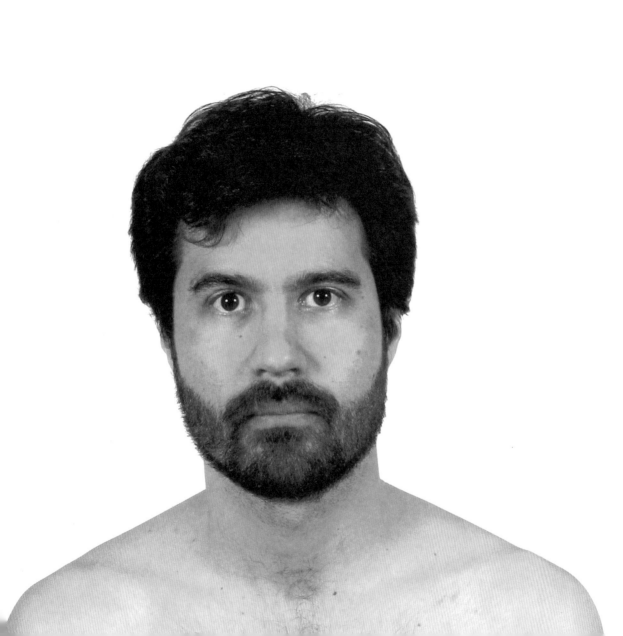

samoan, danish, german, irish

112

IM AN STUDENT / ATHLETE W/ A LARGE FAMILY
I HAVE 2 SISTERS AND 3 BROTHERS. AND
AM EVERYDAY SURROUNDED BY MANY COUSINS
I HAVE 3 VERY CLOSE COUSINS AND ABOUT
25 OTHERS. I LOVE AT THAT IVE BEEN RAISED
WITH AND AROUND MY COUSINS MY WHOLE
LIFE. I LOVE GOING TO THE BEACH TO
BOOYBOARD, CHECK OUT GIRLS, AND CHECK OUT
GIRLS.

114

I am an athlete - physically, mentally and emotionally. I am a bunch of contradictions: fun, yet sincere, carefree, yet responsible, open, yet rigid, simple, yet complex, out-going, yet private, goofy, yet intense. I love life and never get bored. I'm too curious.

When people see my last name, they first ask how to pronounce it and then ask what kind of name it is. When I say Filipino, they look at me and always ask what else.

116

This morning I thought I was going to the movies. Then my mom made me come here.

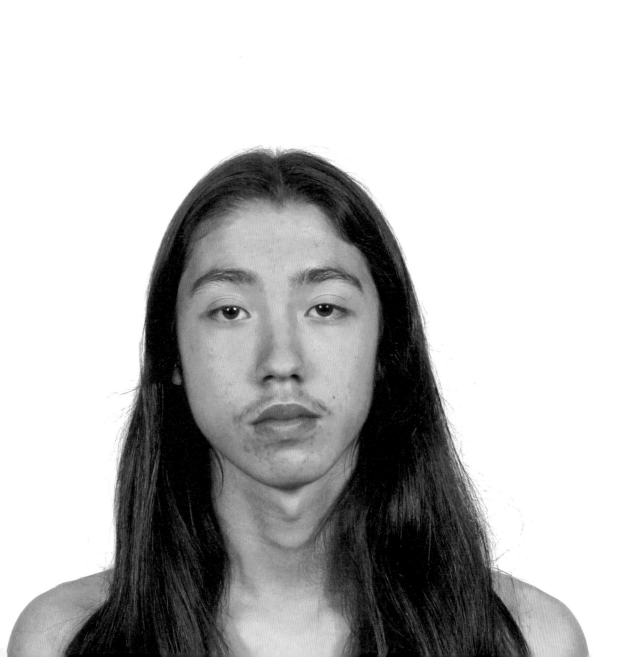

japanese, czechoslovakian, german, english, scottish, irish

I'm a kid who should be able to stay home by myself. There are the reasons why:
1) I won't blow up the hase.
2) I won't get slurpees every day.
3) I won't throw parties

I also like to write, "BOB" on garage sale signs and say random stuff. When I'm at home I'm on the computer or playing videogames.

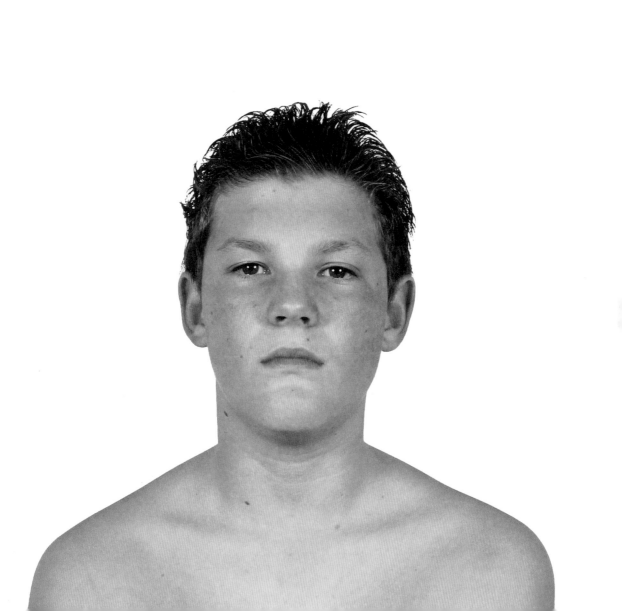

Naturally I feel just a bit different every day. A little older, wiser maybe. Sometimes more Japanese. Sometimes I just gotta have a sauna and some buttered bread. Whatever I feel about myself, its always good. I always feel lucky to be who I am.

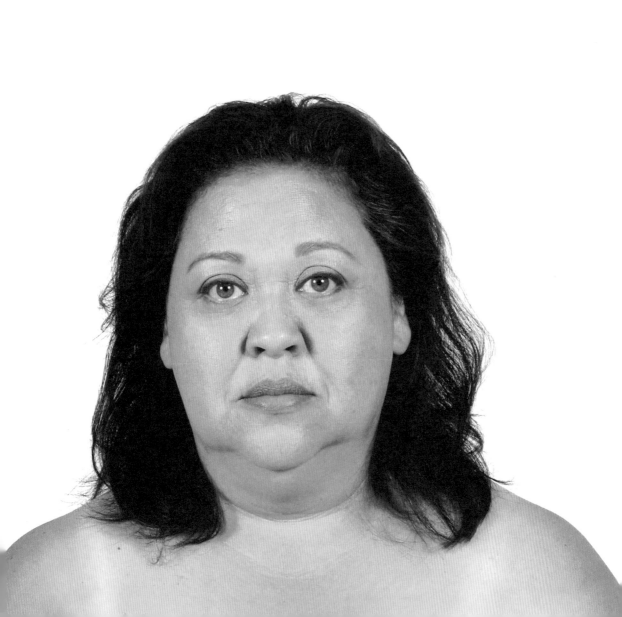

122

I am diverse, happy, confident, silly, a leader, and generally a cool chica!

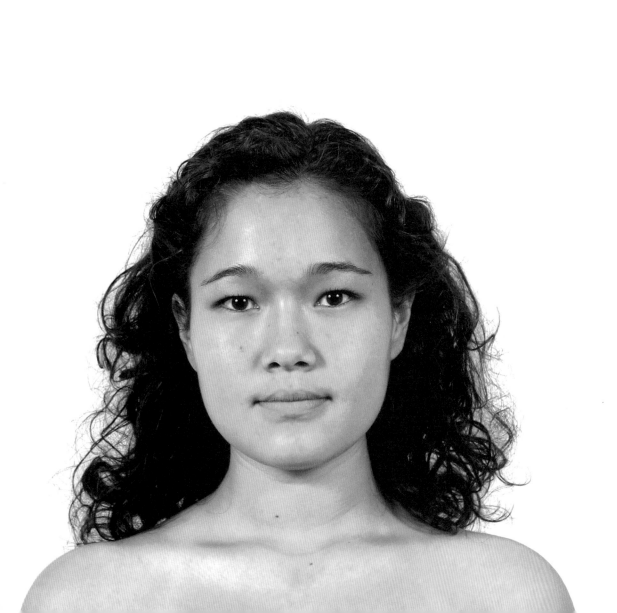

Chinese, Palauan and Austrian. Chinese and what? Palau... its an island nation between Guam and the Philipines. If I only had a dollar for every time I had to explain that. Oh well, at least they cared enough to hear my explaination.

ghanaian, chinese, croatian, scottish, irish, german, indian, british, native american

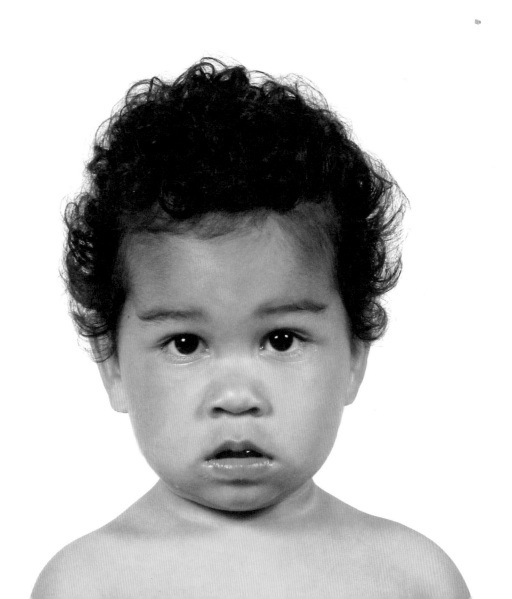

128

I'm all mixed up. I am a runner, although people try to tell me differently. I am a student, I guess. I am an adventurer, although I have not been on any hardcore adventures... yet. I am confused as to what I want to be. As long as it has running and adventure I think I should be good. Maybe ~~biking~~ and adventure. I always tell people if I ever live in a ginourmous city I will be a bicycle messanger. ~~like on the way to~~ the photo shoot I liked to, and it was adventeruous. I almost got hit by a car on Sunset. I yelled at the woman, and I think I ruined her day, even though she made mine by giving me adventure.

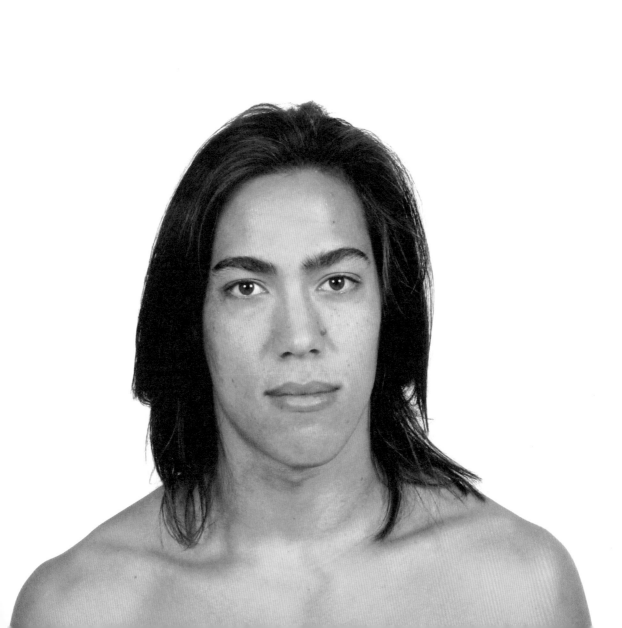

130

I try to just stay calm & say Im from the Bronx. The First Natives of the Americas came across the Bering Strait From Asia about 35,000 years ago. My ancestral Tribe, the Taino, was exterminated by Columbus & Co.. If we'd have seen it coming, we would've Eaten them.

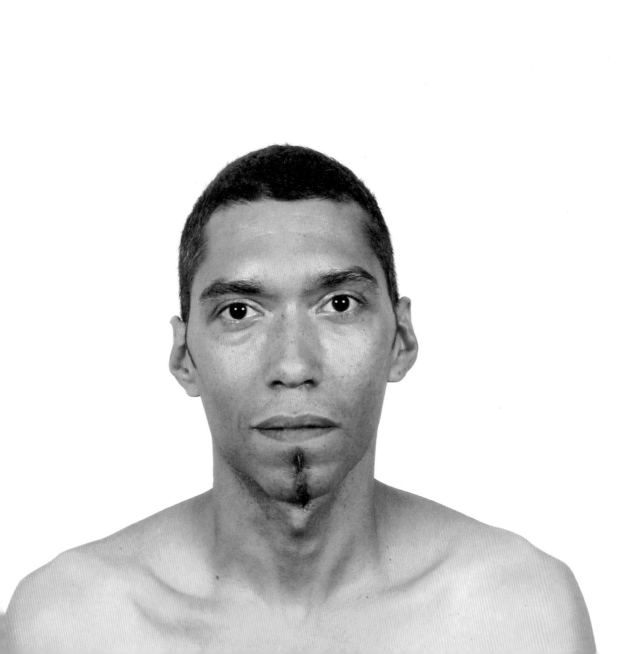

japanese, irish, scottish, german, choctaw

what are you?

~~A daughter of~~

a daughter of God. No one understands me but Him

~~only He understand me~~

I like Brds
I to The shop my mom shop

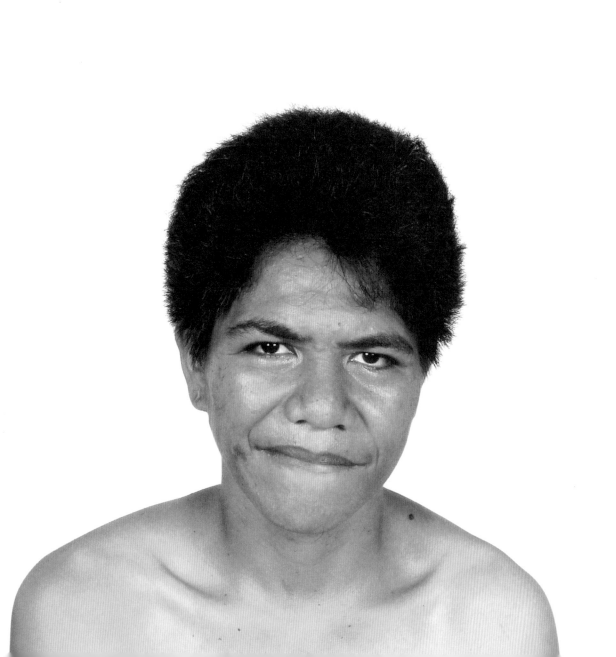

korean, hungarian, irish, german

136

~~[scribbled out]~~
like   snowboarding, skiing, and snowblading!
~~don't like~~ and my 100% Korean Grandmother.
I ~~like being~~ ~~[scribbled out]~~
~~Being~~ in School

hawaiian, chinese, japanese, korean, norwegian, irish, portuguese

HI MY NAME IS JAMES I AM 100% FILIPINO I HAVE SPANISH IN ME, (WHEN THE SPINARDS WENT TO CONQUERED THE PHILIPPINES) I WILL ~~REA~~ ALWAY REPRESENT THE FILIPINO CULTURE.

japanese, german

142

When I was a kid, I was teased for being "different", but when I got older it was the best thing that ever happened to me. When I have my baby girl in a few months, I will teach her to be very proud of being "hapa-hapa-haole". ☺

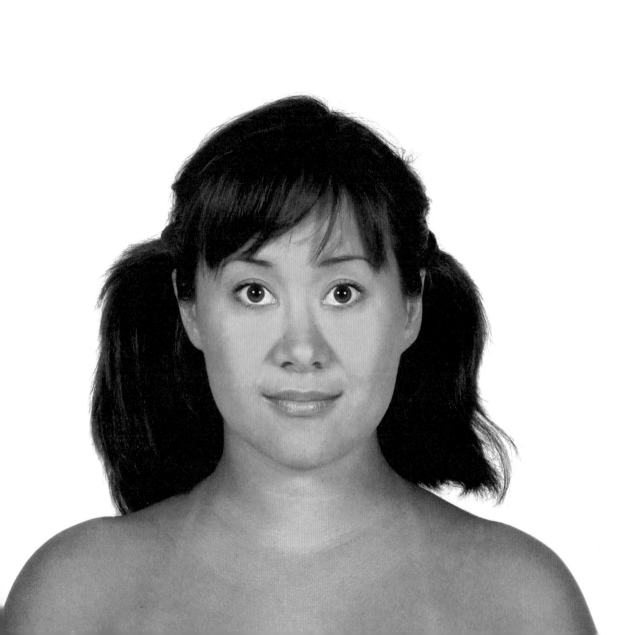

scottish, irish, english, dutch, german, samoan

144   THE EXPERIENCE KNOWN AS " JOE " ☺

What I am? Shouldn't you be telling me that? People tell me I'm "white" b/c I "look white." But then others say they can see the Japanese in me after I tell them. They say, "Oh, I can see it in your eyes!" Where does that leave me? I'm getting conflicting messages. No one questions my father's race or ethnicity. But suddenly, one generation later, I'm not "asian"?

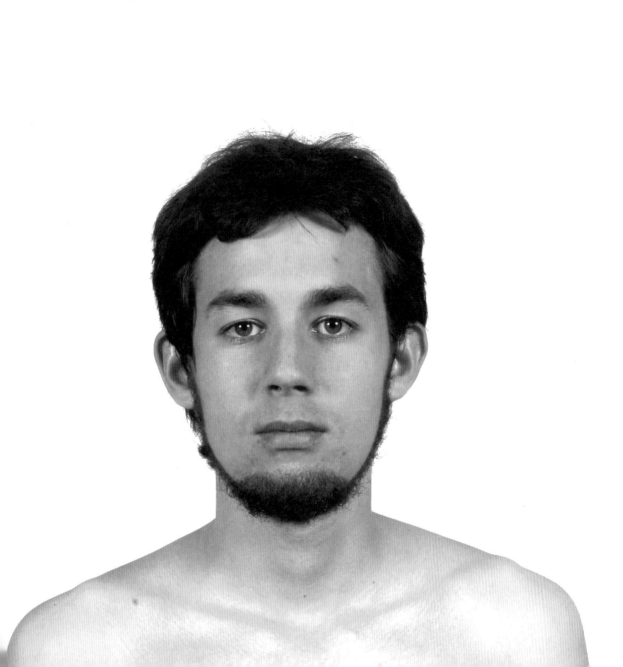

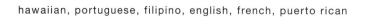

hawaiian, portuguese, filipino, english, french, puerto rican

148

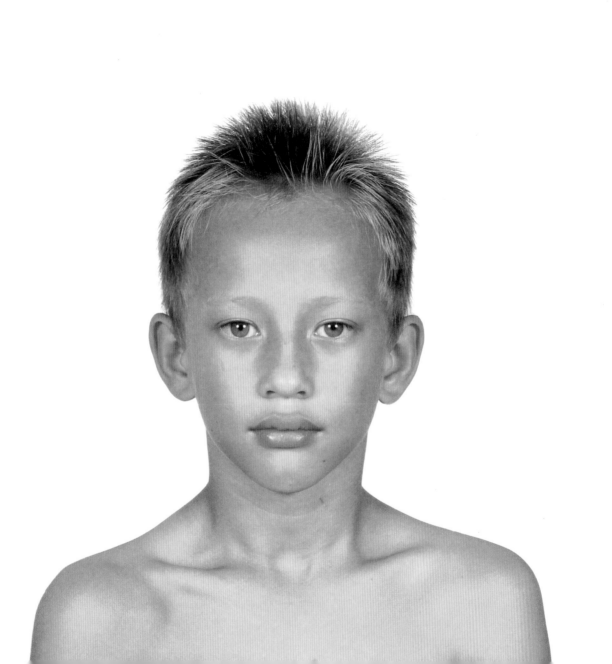

150 I am athletic, I am fun. I love to surf. I am just like you, just a lot shorter.

What am I? Shouldn't you be asking my name first?

chinese (toisan), jewish (russian, polish)

I'm a Hapa Buddhist.
Ever since I came to L.A., I've been working in the
Buddhist community to bring together the "Asians" and the
"Americans." (They don't like to mix.) The best part is
working with the kids. They don't care if I'm Asian or
Caucasian. They just want to know "if I'm chill." Some
days, the kids are my only friends — the only ones who
don't see me as being "on the other side."

filipina, japanese, german

~ I am filipino, Japanese, & german.

~ I am just another teen trying to be herself
& trying to be accepted ~~because~~ because
I know I'm different.

~ I am different, unique, ~~weird~~ wierd, mixed,
myself.

156

158

My last boyfriend told me
he liked me because of my race.
So I dumped him.

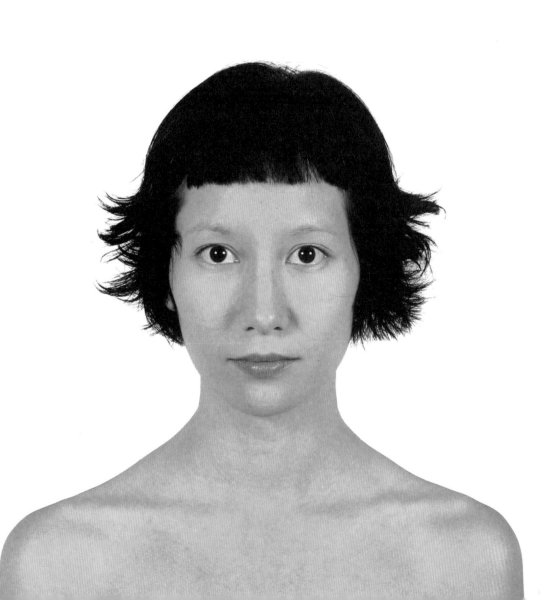

160

Many of my ex-girlfriends were habitual half-asian daters. These women considered half-asian men "exotic", "sexy," and "just-like-Keanu Reeves-in-the-Matrix."

I consider these stereotypes appropriate because I got laid.

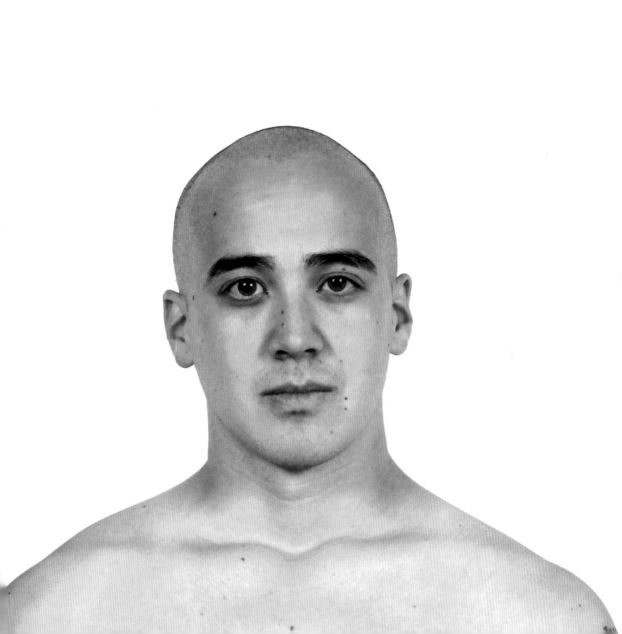

dutch, indonesian, french, german

162

I AM CHARLES BARKLEY TO MY FAMILY, MONTEL WILLIAMS, TO MY FRIENDS, AFRICAN AMERICAN TO THE POLICE, AND BALDY TO MY WIFE.

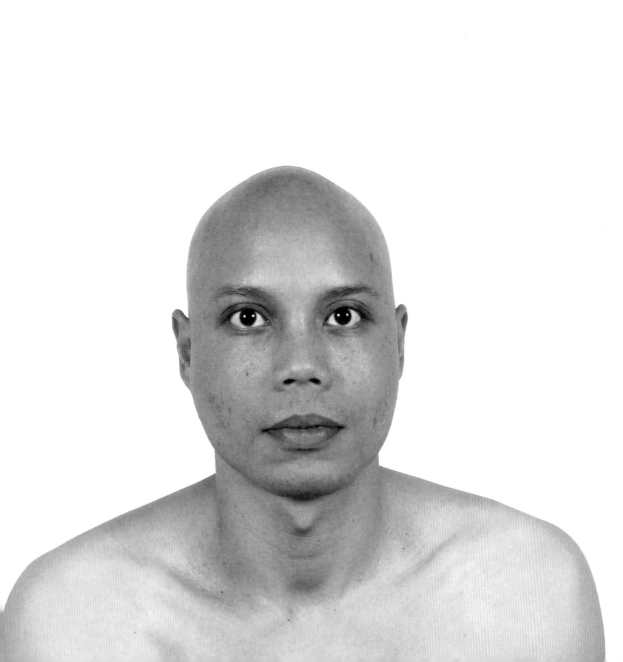

japanese, french, cherokee, irish

I am millions of particles fused together making up a far less than perfect masterpiece. I am the big bang.

guamanian, filipino

166   I AM A FAMILY MAN / PEOPLE PERSON

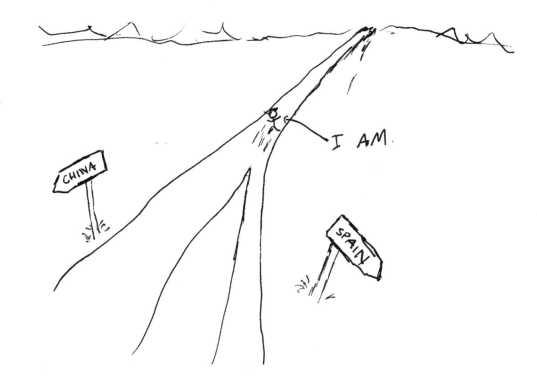

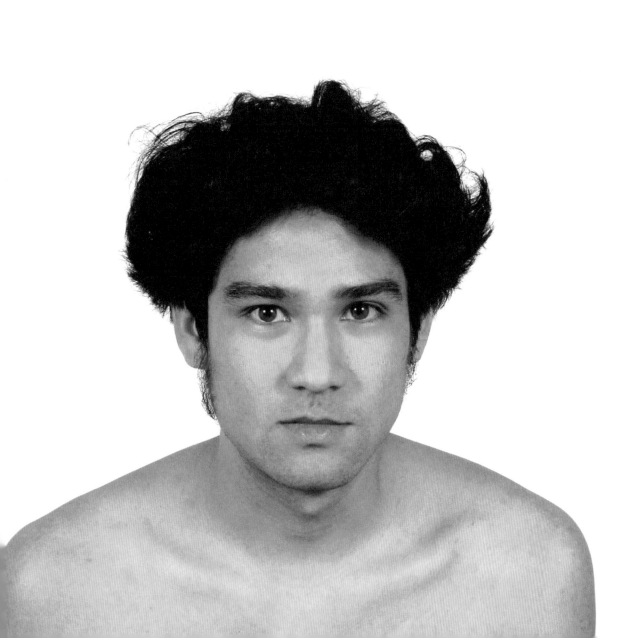

170 I'm a very Littel boy in 5th grade that has nofrands.

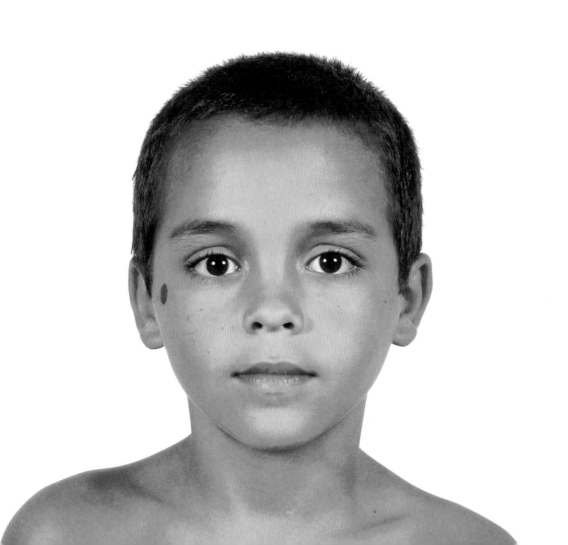

172

Happy to be Hawaiian; there's not many
of us left.

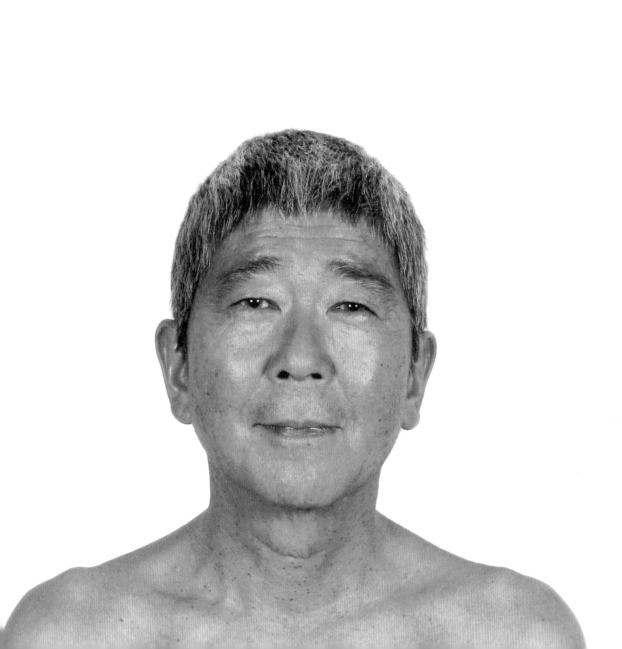

174

Some days I'm very Malay. Other days I'm more "white", American, whatever. But on certain special days, I'm

both.

Those are the best.

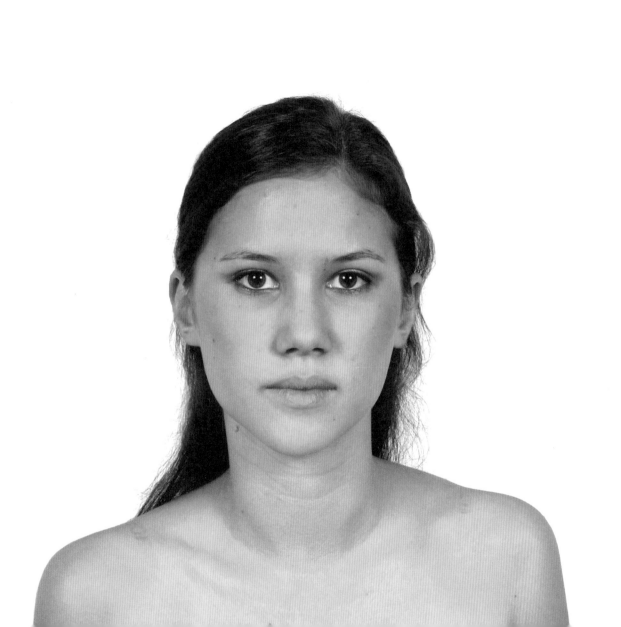

176

My mom cooks really good Indian food. my dad, who is european. he claims to be able to cook all kinds of food, although it tastes more like leather. I hope I'm not what I eat.

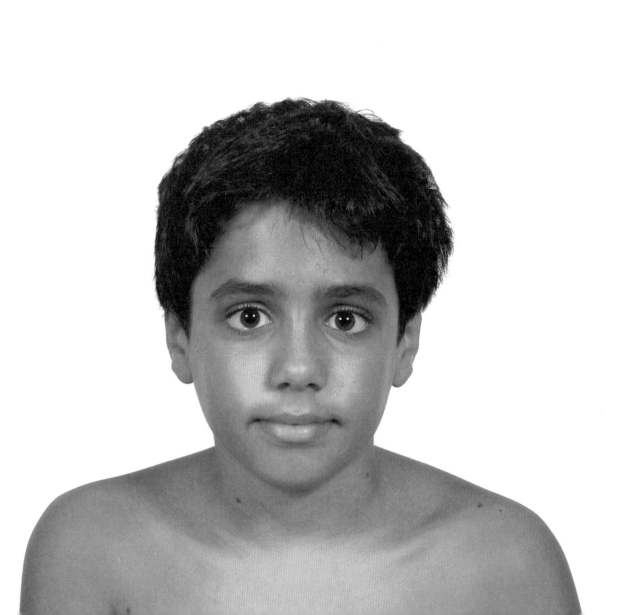

178

Hunggan, Chamorro yan Filipino
Yo'.... I am chamorro and Filipino,
from the island of Saipan. I am
an artist or at least trying to be...
Someday...One day...

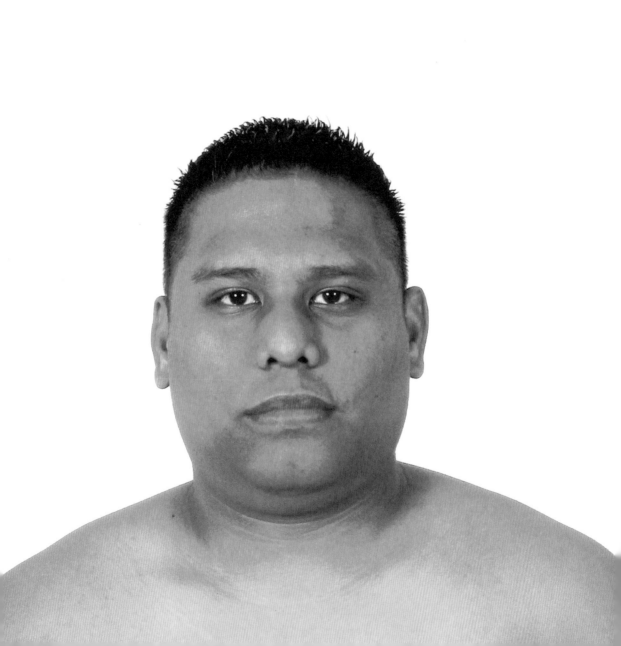

filipina, french

180

I am a unique individual / born from a loving union between two courageous & caring people who saw the inner essence of eachother rather than the labels.
I discovered early in life that I had to identify what I wanted to be as a person, in order to survive the hurtful assaults from the 'labelers'.
This is what I continually strive to be & the way I live my life . . .
- Treat others as one wants to be treated - be kind, respectful, caring, sharing & loving
- Care about & respect oneself, others, & all living things.
- Be responsible for one's actions.
- Leave a place better than it was before one got there.
- Listen to the 'rhythms of life', identify the 'messages' & respond in a positive way to develop quality interactions & foster mutual understanding
- Live life fully & generously
- Understand & accept people for their qualities, characteristics & actions
- Set goals, develop action strategies to achieve those goals, adjust to detours / setbacks, redirect focus, & complete the tasks necessary to achieve those goals.
This is within my realm of control. This is what I look for in others.

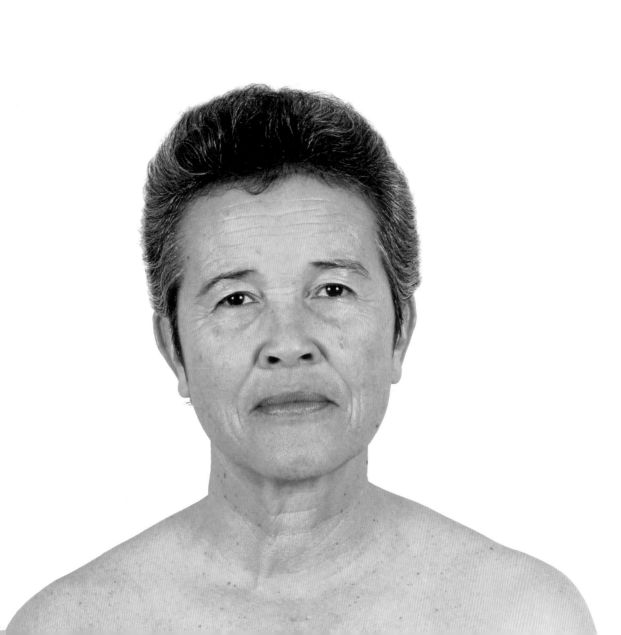

chinese, wasp

182 QUEER EURASIAN

184

I get this question everytime I go ~~Dancing~~.
"what are you" I pretend not to understand
the question, because I am so sick ~~of it~~.
From black people I get, "I knew you were part
Asian!" From Asians, they tell me they didn't
know I was part asian. I just feel I am
who I am. PERIOD.

186

I AM CHINESE

SHANGAI DAD

MET IN
SOUTHERN
CALIFORNIA
IN THE
'50s

GERMAN

HE HAD A SNAZZY
BUICK, SHE
NEEDED A RIDE
HOME FROM
THE CALTECH
POOL! NOW

DANZIG MOM

POLAND

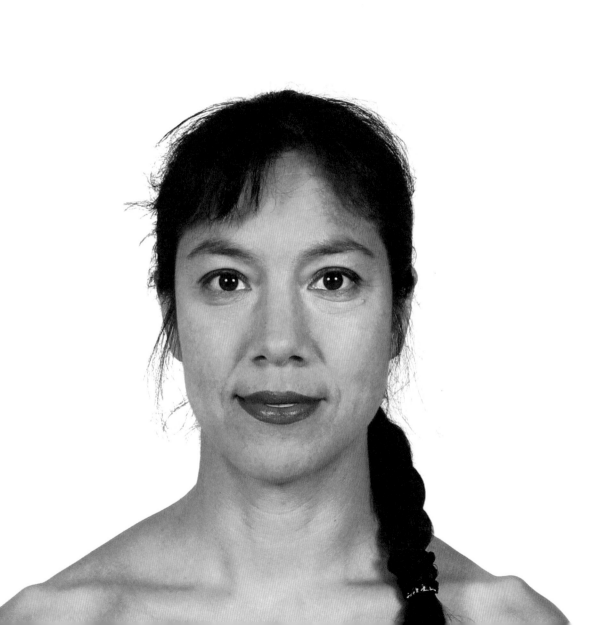

I am mixed. I like playing with my friends. When I get older I want to be a star. I really like sports.

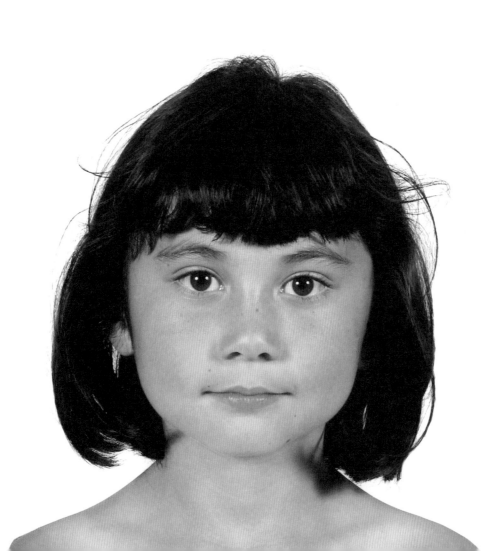

I AM A MONSTER! RAA!!
AND I HAVE A PET DRAGON..... ← QUAIL
WELL... I'M ACTUALLY A PEPSI TWIST. NO...
I'M A DARK, DARK BLACK HOLE THAT SUCKS THE
UNIVERSE.

190

I'M AN ALIEN! (WITH PINK SNEAKERS!)

Woman
Daughter
Adoptee
AIDS   Orphan
Hapa
Japanese
American
Japanese - American
Asian
Asian - American
Queer
Musician
Writer
Martial Artist
Alive

I am not who
you think I am.

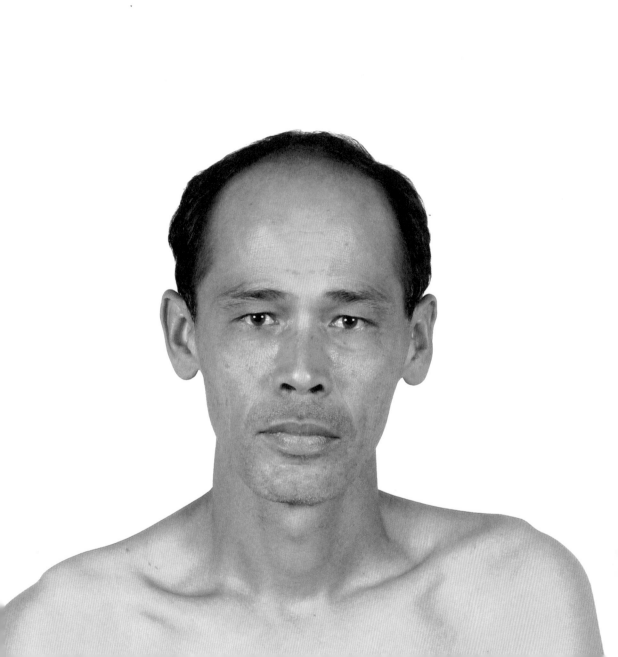

I Am a Young Man that loves football & baseball and doesnt really care about that many things. That doent Counsern me unless it is Someone I know. I Also love the beach ▬ and Surfing and cares about a girl and I will never hit one

198

I am the Jewish daughter of a Catholic father.
I am the tan sister of a white brother.
I am the actor with both the romantic lead monologue
& the ethnic monologue in her back pocket.
I have been Persian, Mexican, Assyrian, mestiza &
the girl with a good tan.
I come from all groups. I am a member of
anything if one person thinks so.
I am fortunate.

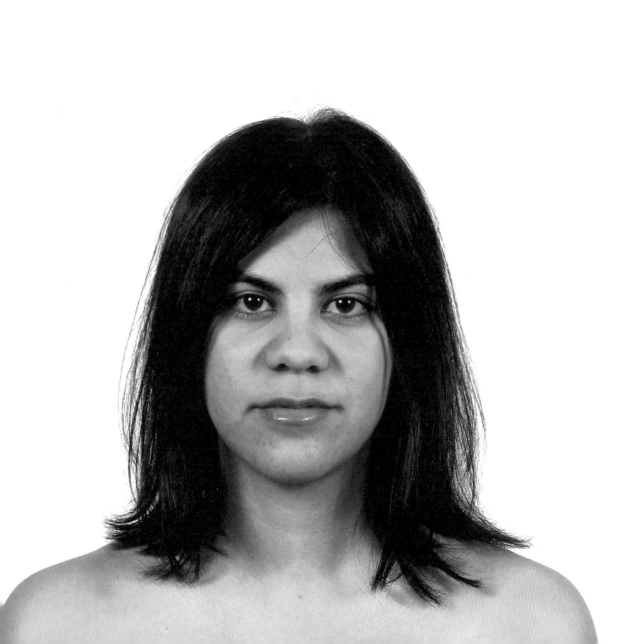

200

No. Spain never colonized Viet Nam.
But, thanks for asking.
I am a scholar, organizer & adventurer.
I strive for unique thoughts with
universal understandings - precisely because
it is expected of me &
not expected of me.

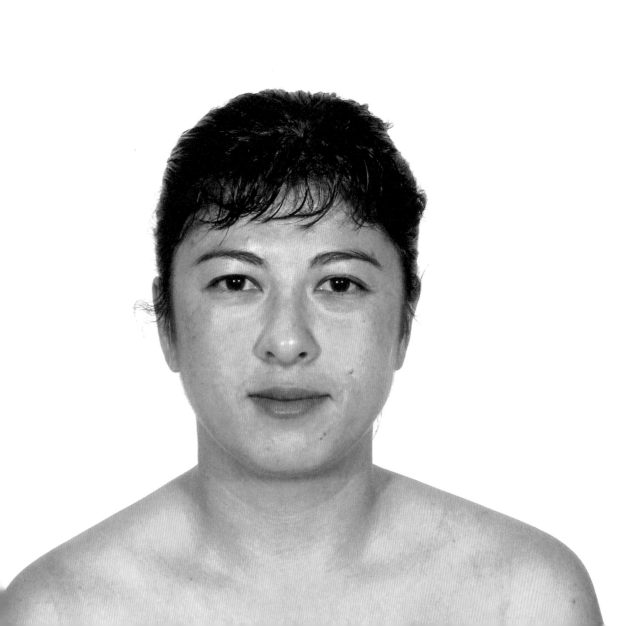

202

I'M 6'7" OF LOVE.

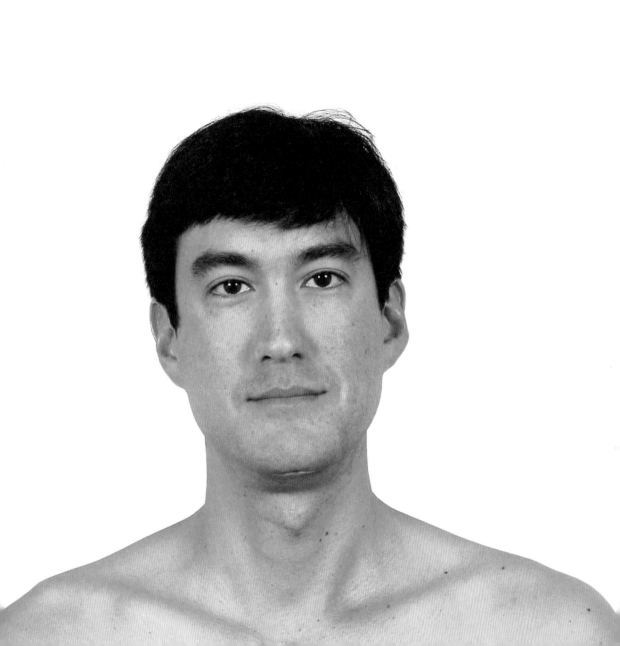

204 Ambiguous, bad at spelling, confused, anserine, other, brown.

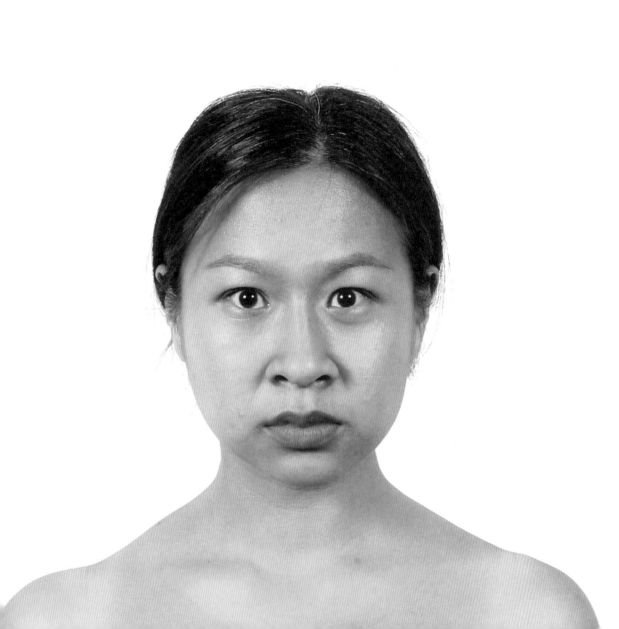

thai, chinese, norwegian, irish

206 *why? ... Are you coming on to me?*

208

I AM A CROSSBRED, CROSS DRESSING, ROCK GOD GUITARIST, I WAS IN A BAND WITH MY BROTHER AND COUSINS AND AFTER THE SHOW SOME PEOPLE CAME UP TO ME AND ASKED IF WE WERE JAPANESE. MY REPLY WAS "NO CHICO SOMOS CUBANOS"

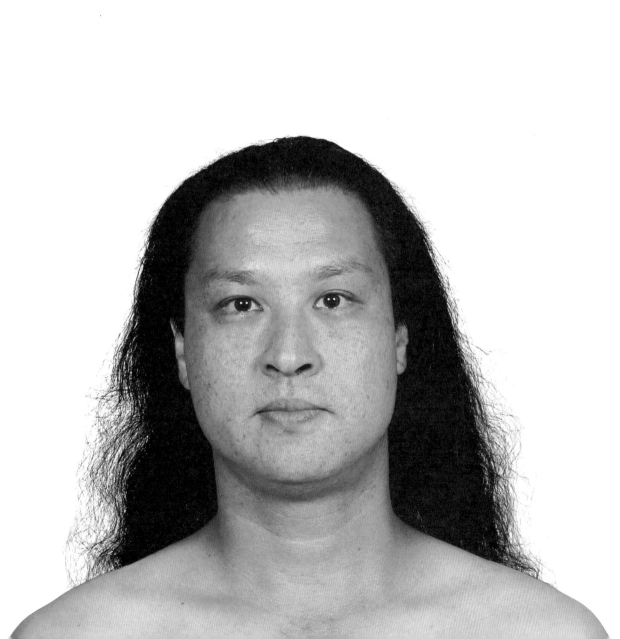

hakka, shanghainese, welsh, english, german, swiss

ONE BAD ASS SISTA!
WHO ARE YOU?

210

one hiphapa from the BAY!
½ hapa ½ oakland

hawaiian, chinese, german, japanese

212

mom

Evan

Audrey

Rad

Shay

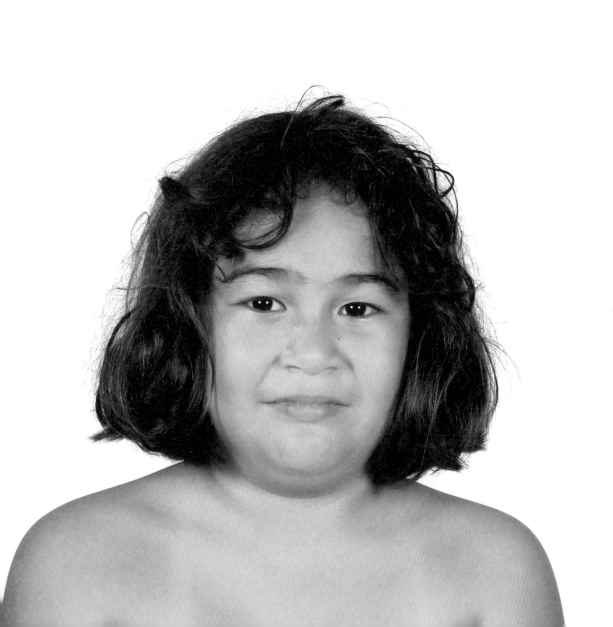

214

I'm a mestiza. I joke that my mother is Japanese, my father is Anglo + I'm Mexican - that's how the world has identified me since I came to California from Pakistan at age 8. I love not having a specific racial, cultural or even gender identity. Life is fluid + richly all-encompassing when you don't have restrictions stamped on ~~your~~ the passport of self-perception.

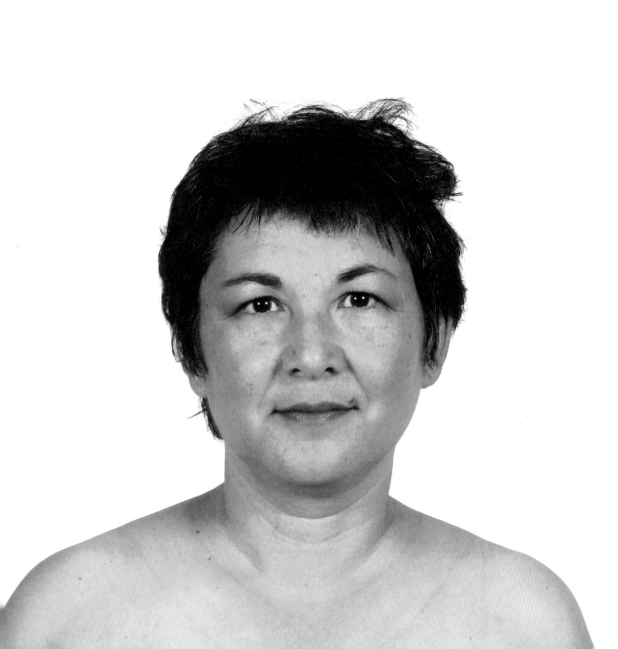

japanese, jewish (russian)

WHAT ARE YOU? HARD TO SAY, EXCEPT MAYBE SELF-
CONTAINED, LEFTIST AND HUMOROUS ... AND
INCREASINGLY IMPATIENT WITH THE NONSENSE
OF OTHERS?

ACTUALLY, THE REASON THIS IS HARD BECAUSE I'M
USED TO DEFINING MYSELF, AND BEING DEFINED,
MOSTLY BY WHAT I'M NOT. I <u>AM</u> A FATHER. ALL
OTHER CLAIMS TO ~~INDIVIDUALITY~~ SEEM FLUID OR
DEPENDENT ON THE CONTEXT. MAINLY, IT SEEMS
THAT I AM WHAT OTHERS ARE NOT.

IS HAPA ENOUGH FOR YOU?

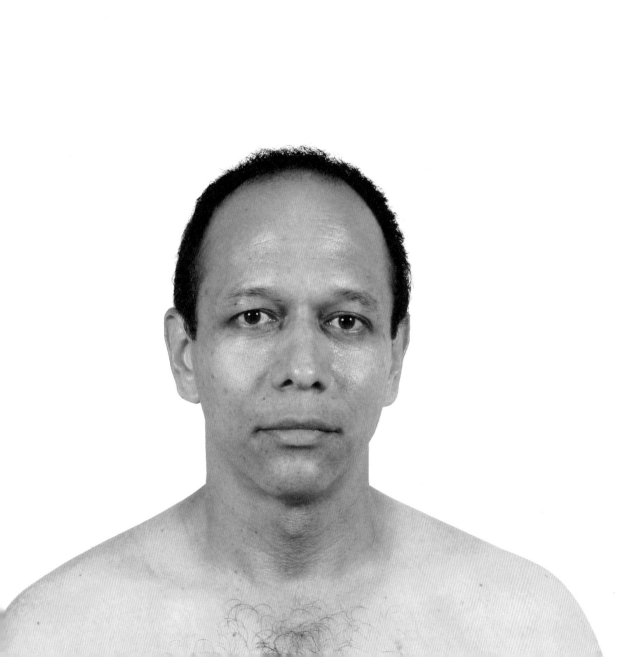

hawaiian, chinese, german, japanese

I am GODDESS
I am WOMAN -
ConfiDent o Arrogant

People always speak to me in spanish because they think I'm latino. Of course my spanish is much better than my non-existant chinese.

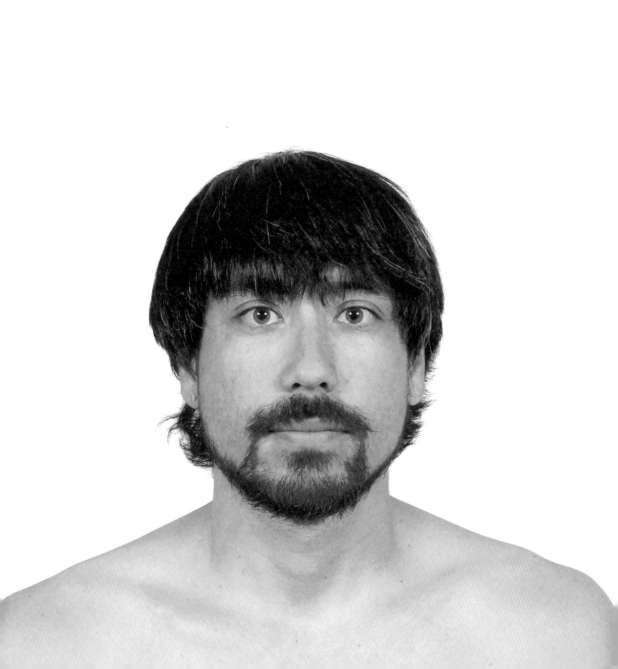

226

I am as complex as any other person. It is a rare label that can describe me without its opposite also being true.

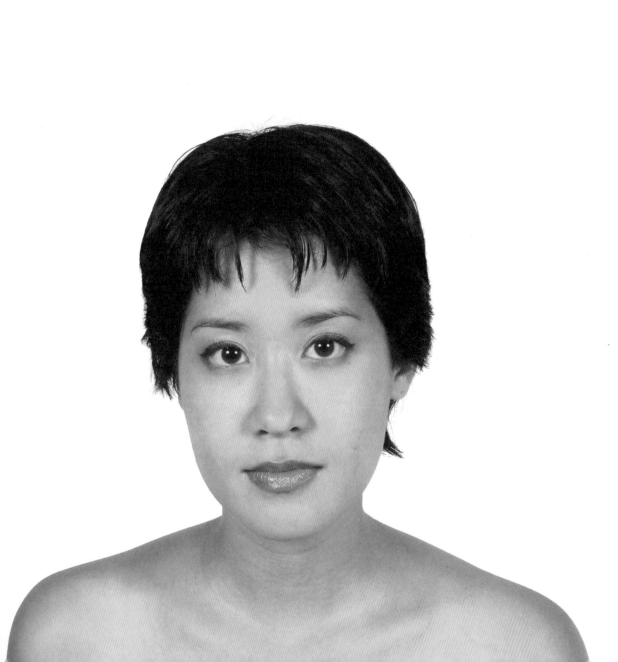

228 *I am whatever you want when you want it*

230

I'm the guy who says and does whatever he wants because whoever I'm with, white or asian, says to himself, "It's okay, he's half."

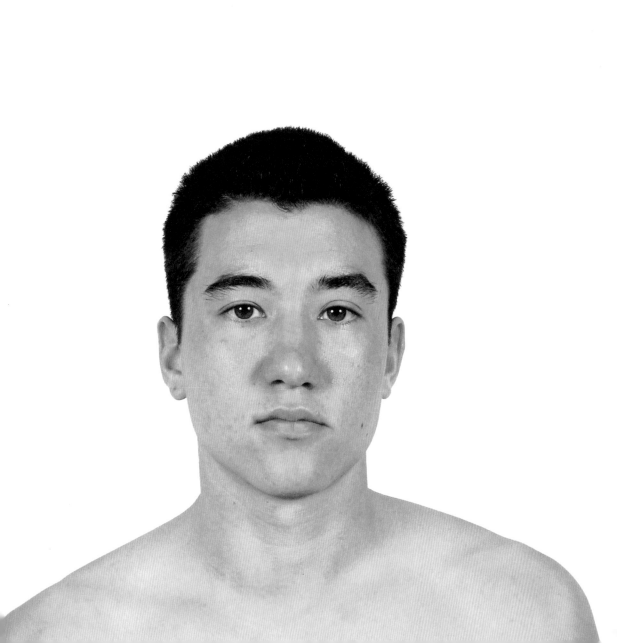

chinese, greek, swedish, english, scottish, german, pennsylvania dutch

232

I am an Asian American Hapa Activist Academic Artist. I can't count how many times I have been asked "What Are You?" – I am not EXOTIC or FOREIGN I am more than the Sum of my Parts – I am part of a growing Hapa Community.

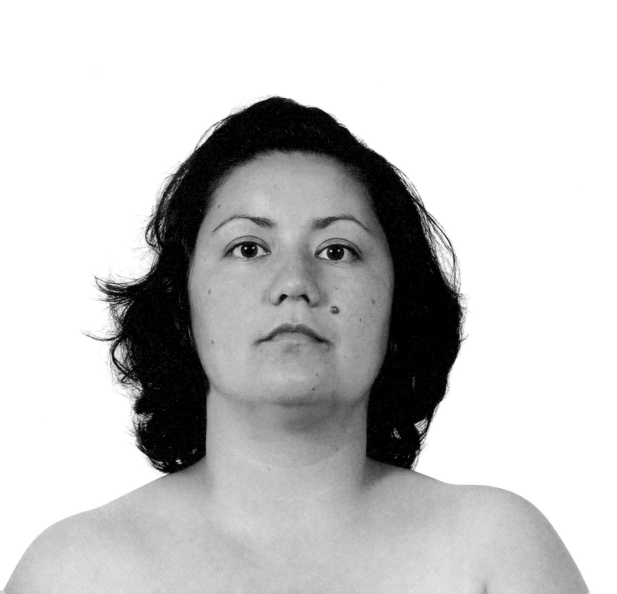

SANSEI A GENERATION. MANY OF OUR PARENTS OVEREACTED AFTER THE INTERNMENT AND DIDN'T TEACH US THE LANGUAGE OR CUSTOMS OF JAPAN. NOT QUITE JAPANESE, NOT QUITE AMERICAN. MOST OF MY FRIENDS AND CO-WORKERS KNOW ME ONLY AS "ICHIBAN". A PATRIOT, A STRONG SUPPORTER AND TRUE BELIEVER IN THE GREATEST COUNTRY IN THE WORLD THE UNITED STATES OF AMERICA.

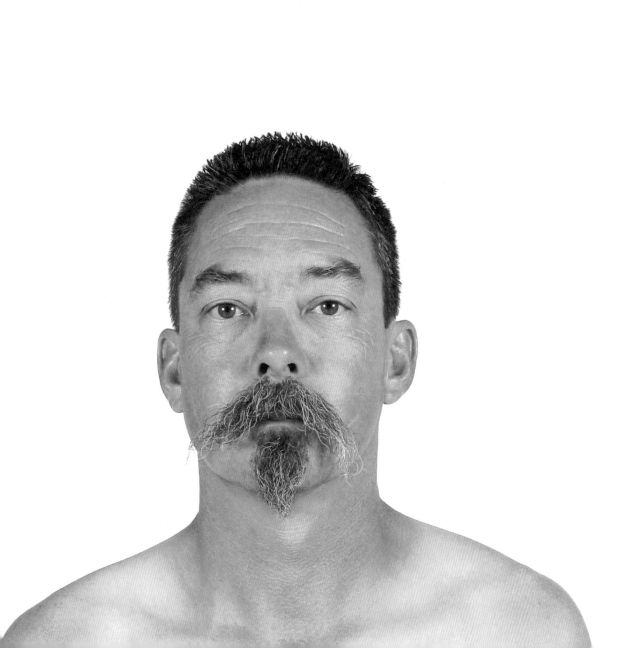

scottish, irish, french, swedish, hawaiian, chinese

238

boy Elijah purple belt

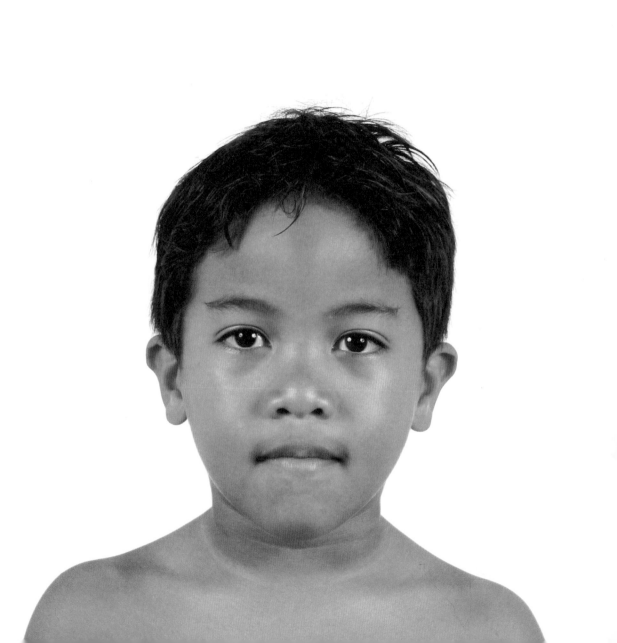

japanese, scottish

240

I am a retired University professor of chemistry, retired since 1981 but still doing some consulting work. Came to USA in 1919 from Japan,

I, my wife, our five children, and three grandchildren are truly "citizens of the world."

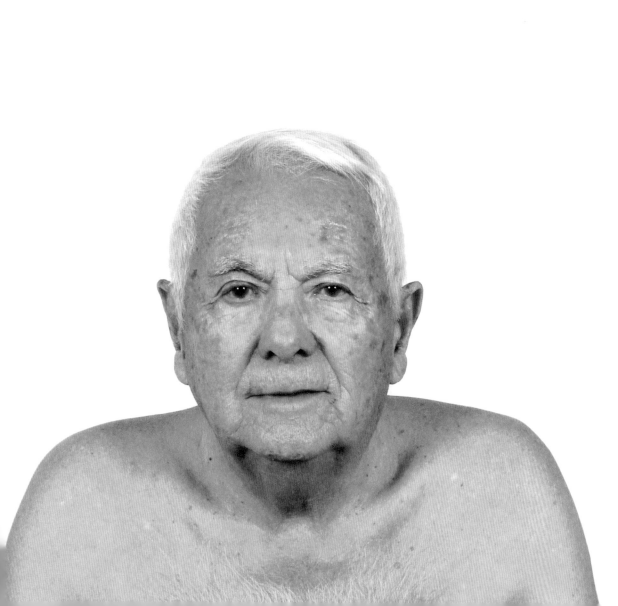

korean, argentinian

242 I'm a lover not a fighter.

244

I'm ~~special~~ special. My dad is Black, and my mom is Thai. I've lived with my dad since I was 2. I haven't spoken with my mom since then, but nontheless I am asian. I don't really know anything about my Thai culture, but I still take pride in it. When I'm asked about my race, I say that I am Black & Thai. I am not one or the other. I am both, and I shouldn't have to choose. ~~It doesn't really~~
~~matter~~

chinese, german, dutch, british

246

I'M A CHINESE THAT CAN'T DO MATH. I'M A WHITE GUY
THAT EATS WITH CHOPSTICKS. I'M A GUY WHO LOOKS
JUST LIKE SOMEONE YOU KNOW, JUST LIKE HIM.
MY ROLE MODELS ARE HONG KONG PHOOEY, BRUCE
LEE, AND STEVE McQUEEN.

I CONVINCED THE OTHER KIDS IN MY ELEMENTARY
SCHOOL THAT I KNEW KUNG FU, SO NO ONE
FUCKED WITH ME. I DON'T KNOW KUNG FU.

I am
100% Black
and 100%
Japanese

250

I'm 53, ~~older tha~~
2nd generation HAPA, older than most
people I know who identify as mixed-Asian.
Lacking people to identify with slowed
me down. I'm still trying to finish college —
got married too late to have kids. My husband
is African-American — a group that does
Know how to Relate to Racially mixed people.
I live in the SF Bay Area. It's paradise
for someone like me. Took me til I was
30 to get here. Then life Really started! ~~████~~

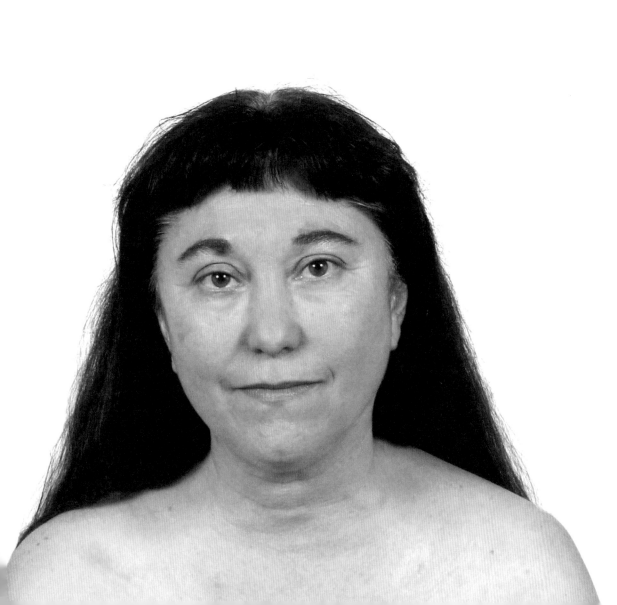

chinese, jamaican, african american, dutch, norwegian

Multiracial and Proud!

254

I am a person of color.
I am not half- "white".
I am not half - "Asian".
I am a whole "other".

☑ other

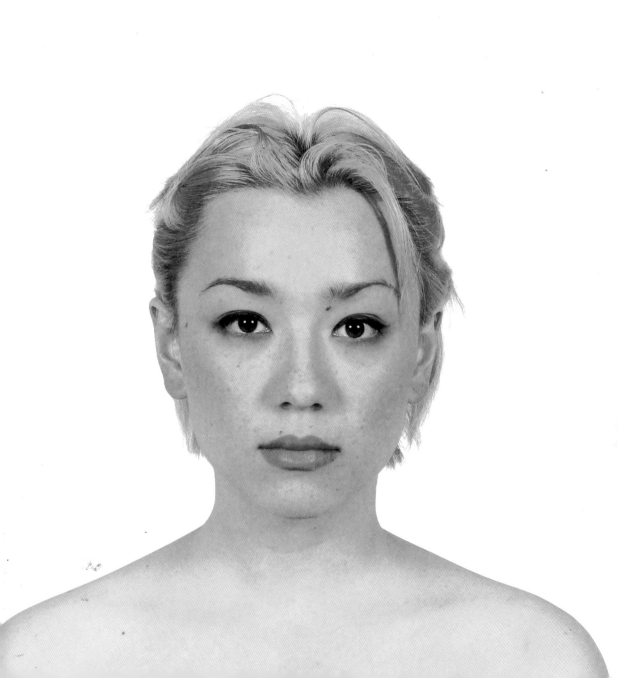

afterword | paul spickard

Somewhere in my twenties, I picked up a book that changed my life—*Mixed Blood: An Examination of Intermarriage and Ethic Identity* by Paul Spickard. Now, I'm not a big-time academic (despite my university moniker), being much more comfortable exploring pop culture than reading critical theory. But I found Professor Spickard's writing smart and insightful without trying to sound smart and insightful—a tough call when you're one of the world's preeminent scholars on race/ethnicity and the author of dozens of books and articles. Through this book, I was introduced to a colleague and field of study that affected me on a personal level, helping to form my own research and art practice. Now entering my fourth decade, I'm proud to call Paul a trusted friend and adviser. I asked him to write this conclusion for *Part Asian, 100% Hapa*.

— Kip Fulbeck

"It's always been our time." Those are the last words of the introduction to this book. And they are true. Hapas, racially mixed people, have always been around. We are *all* mixed. Every so-called racial group—no matter how "pure" it thinks it is—has multiple ancestries. Go check your family tree. You will find ancestors you did not know were there.

That we are all mixed has always been true. What is new these days is that people are owning up to being mixed. The people whose pictures and words are in this book are owning up to it. A lot of the people reading this book are mixed, and the pictures and words may help them own up to it as well. There is something freeing in that, something celebrating.

I expect that readers of this book will have been entranced by the images they have seen and the self-descriptions they have read. But it is possible that a few readers may have misinterpreted a couple of issues. So I would like to address those possible misconceptions briefly.

Misinterpretation 1. *Hapa*—the Web site, the project, the book—shows pictures of people's shoulders and faces without much expression or any clothes or jewelry. Accompanying each picture are some words about that person's ancestries.

Some readers might think that framing the subjects of the photographs this way is making more or less the same move that racist so-called scientists made half a century ago, when they put pictures like that and racial fractions like that in their books. They tried to measure the mixture of race in each person by measuring their noses and eye folds and skin tones. They thought they could measure who people were by their shapes and colors.

For those "scientists," people of color did not have individual identities or stories, and they did not get to speak for themselves. They were just racial equations like "half-Chinese, one-quarter Polynesian, one-quarter

European." Those books treated racially mixed people as if they were exhibits in human zoos.

That was racist nonsense, but this book is doing something quite different. Kip Fulbeck is using the pictures to provoke and encourage his readers. He is using the old form, but with exactly opposite content. Every one of his subjects has an identity and a story. Every one gets to speak for him or herself, and gets to define him or herself however he or she wants to. That is taking the old racist trope and turning it on its head.

Misinterpretation 2. The book begins with a definition of "Hapa." A few misguided people might object to that usage. Hapa started out as a Hawaiian word that means "half." It was used before about 1960 in the term "Hapa Haole." In that usage, it referred to people who had White (Haole) and Hawaiian ancestry. In those days, Hapa Haoles formed a middle class between Haoles and Hawaiians.

But Hawai`i is a place where a lot of people are mixed, and not just with Haoles and Hawaiians. There are people who are Japanese and Chinese, Korean and Filipino, Portuguese and Black and Samoan, and a lot of other things, too. By the 1970s, Hapa was being used by everybody in Hawai`i to refer to anyone who was mixed. Then Asians from the continental United States visited their relatives in Hawai`i and brought the word back home with them. And they started applying it to anybody who was mixed and part Asian.

I sympathize with resentments some Hawaiians may have at their word being appropriated by Asian Americans. But that is the nature of language. It morphs and moves. It is not anyone's property. Continental Americans might just as well complain about Hawaiians using "TV" and "cell phone."

The Hawaiian origins of the word Hapa are worthy of respect. The people in this book use the term respectfully. That is all that anyone can ask.

These pictures and stories are rich with meaning, emotion, and possibility. Now is the Hapa time.

featured participants

JoJo Alepuyo	Helgi Jonsson	Greg Pak
Tygue Allport	Audrey Kauwe	Joseph Paleafei
Gregg Alzate	Evan Kauwe	David Pon
Tyrone Aquino	Keith Kauwe	Windy Pua
Kristen Baggerly	Laura Kina	Noelani Ranoa
Lynda Barry	Kyle Kryska	Yoji Reichert
Niah Bernardo	Dan Kwong	Kate Rigg
Wuv Bernardo	Aaron Lee	Camille Rockett
Scott Brown	Elizabeth Leidelmeijer	Stephanie Ropp
Stephen Brown	Robert Leidelmeijer	Jan Rowan
Asia Carrera	Ronnie Leidelmeijer	Sonny Sandoval
Olivia Castillon	Fiona Lennstrom	Chiori Santiago
Sheila Chung	Ryan Lien	Jonathan Sass
Erika Clement	Donna Ligutom-Kimura	Kassie Sass
Jenn Crawford	Erica Lord	Emily Shin
Hanna Cruz	Kim Lucas	Janet Siharath
Andrew Dabney	Sunida Maclachlan	Kelly Smith
Wei Ming Dariotis	Gaby Mark	Nolan Spencer
Elijah Dasher	Reed Maruyama	Daniel Spickard
Karen David	Liz Masakayan	Kevin Tam
Daniel Delgado	Kiran Mathrani	Rhena Tantisunthorn
Yes Duffy	Myrna McCune	Eric Tate
Amy Evenson	Shea McNanie	Tom Thomson
Catalina Freitas	Sophia Means	Randi Thomson-Story
Stuart Gaffney	Quinn Messmer	Charlise Tiee
Pilar Garcia-Brown	Madeline Loh Miller	Sandra Tsing Loh
Theo Grison	Bernz Mokulehua	Christine Turner
Ikaika Gunderson	Imari Molifua	James Vallejo
Christine Hamilton	Chile Moralls	KieuLinh Valverde
Anne Hawkinson	Adrian Moy	Melissa Van Kirk
Paul Hein	Shane Murphy	Derrick Velasquez
Zachary Helsley	Chris Naka	Carrie Walters
Amy Hill	Paul Nakayama	Doug Watson
Huygen Hilling	Amma Nichols	Nichelle Wentz
Max Hing	Jaden Nichols	Tim Wildin
Teresa Hodges	Jeffrey Norris	Eso Windrem
Sophie Hou	Alisa Ochoa	Michael Wong
Christina Howard	Harper Olmon	Sarah Zain
Joemy Ito-Gates	D.J. Ozan	